FUTURI

Stephen Brown

# FUTURE ME

*Stephen Brown*

OBERON BOOKS
LONDON

First published in 2007 by Oberon Books Ltd
521 Caledonian Road, London N7 9RH
Tel: 020 7607 3637 / Fax: 020 7607 3629
e-mail: info@oberonbooks.com
www.oberonbooks.com

A catalogue record for this book is available from the British
Library.

Cover design by Oberon Books.

ISBN: 1 84002 758 4 / 978-1-84002-758-7

Printed in Great Britain by Antony Rowe Ltd, Chippenham.

# Characters

PETER
29, a lawyer

JENNY
27, Peter's girlfriend, a journalist

MIKE
28, Peter's brother, a computer expert

HARRY
48, a prisoner

ELLEN
40, a probation officer

TIM
50, a prisoner and journalist

PATRICK
35, a prisoner

Ages are approximate and indicate characters'
ages at the start of the play.
The play takes place between 2000 and 2005.

*Future Me* was first performed at Theatre503, London, on 19 June 2007, with the following cast:

PETER,  David Sturzaker

JENNY,  Kelly Williams

MIKE / PATRICK,  Stefan Butler

HARRY,  Philip Fox

ELLEN,  Sara Griffiths

TIM,  David Benson

*Director*  Guy Retallack

*Designer*  Dan Potra

*Lighting Designer*  Mark Truebridge

*Composer*  Leo Chadburn

*Produced by*  Elkie Jeffery
 Sue Scott Davison

# Act One

## THE SWIMMING POOL STORY

*The kitchen of JENNY's flat.*

*The kitchen has recently been replaced. It is compact but well appointed. The work surfaces gleam.*

*It is late at night. There is a bottle of wine on the kitchen table, nearly empty, and two glasses of wine. PETER occasionally drinks.*

*PETER is sat at the table. There is a document in front of him.*

*JENNY is sat at the table. There is a Sunday newspaper magazine in front of her, open.*

*Both are at the end of their twenties, but she is petite and looks younger.*

JENNY: That's weird.

PETER: What?

JENNY: These people have the same swimming pool as my grandparents.

PETER: They all look the same, don't they?

JENNY: No, no. There's a seahorse mosaic on the bottom. Just like theirs. I could have sworn they said some local artist had done it.

*She puts the magazine in front of PETER. He glances up at it for a moment.*

PETER: Maybe they got it out of a catalogue.

JENNY: They didn't get anything out of a catalogue.

PETER: Hmm.

JENNY: I used to love that pool. I was in there for hours every day when we went to stay with them.

You know I found a deer in their pool once.

PETER: (*Choking on wine.*) You what?

JENNY: I found a deer in their pool.

PETER: A deer? A deer deer?

JENNY: As in Rudolph. With antlers. I mean, not a reindeer.

PETER: Was it swimming?

JENNY: Not any more.

PETER: Oh right.

JENNY: It was weirder than that. The thing was, I used to check that pool every morning. It had one of those floating plastic covers, which you put on at night, and every morning there'd be things caught on it. Lots of insects, beetles and then the odd shrew or a hedgehog. I loved it. My granddad would go out there first thing in the morning with a net and scoop everything up. I used to do it with him. And when I was old enough I did it on my own, it was my thing I did. Like a nature project.

PETER: Collecting dead beetles?

JENNY: They weren't all dead. Some of them ran off into the undergrowth. And then you'd saved them.

PETER: But not Rudolph.

JENNY: No. It had this horrible red froth around its nostrils.

PETER: Must have freaked you out.

JENNY: I don't know. It made me a celebrity for a while, amongst the adults, everybody wanting to hear my story. That was good. And when this local farmer came to pull it out, they had to take down part of the fence to get the tractor in. And I took photos of the whole thing. For my scrapbook.

PETER: I think we should agree now never to encourage any of our many children to have an interest in nature. It's unpredictable and strange. They are going to be entirely urban.

JENNY: It was so massive. That was the thing. This huge brown animal against the blue of the pool, all tangled up in the pool cover.

PETER: 'Like a tarantula on a slice of angel cake.'

JENNY: Who's that?

PETER: Raymond Chandler.

JENNY: Right. Like a deer in a swimming pool. It must have thought the pool cover was solid ground, in the moonlight, like a sheet of silver. Then bam! And next morning this snotty-nosed little girl comes along and takes photos of your corpse.

*Beat.*

Well, that's your bedtime story.

PETER: Sweet dreams to you too.

*JENNY has got up and is walking round the table until she is behind PETER.*

JENNY: That means it's bedtime.

*She reaches down and embraces him from behind. Kissing the side of his face.*

PETER: I've got to finish this.

*Suddenly JENNY has snatched the document from in front of him and run around the other side of the table, holding it out of reach.*

JENNY: Come on. I thought they were going to settle anyway.

PETER: I can't assume that. Unfortunately.

JENNY: I think you should come to bed.

*JENNY gives him a look.*

You spend too many nights up working. That's not what the night's for.

PETER: I know.

*Beat.*

PETER: I've been thinking. Maybe you're right. I should put my flat up for rent.

JENNY: Really? What brought this on?

PETER: It's stupid paying for two flats.

JENNY: You're so romantic.

PETER: I could get a lot of money for my flat. And you have this new kitchen. Which I really like.

JENNY: You like my work surfaces?

PETER: It's good to wake up next to you.

JENNY: It's good to wake up next to you. Come on. I'll do you the dance of the seven veils.

*JENNY puts the document back down on the table in front of PETER, absent-mindedly runs her hand through his hair as she walks away.*

PETER: We could build a swimming pool. Could be your birthday present. In a few years.

JENNY: Forty-five seconds. Then I start the dance without you.

PETER: Could you call me when you reach number six?

*She's gone.*

*PETER returns to the document, reads, concentrates.*

*Into:*

## THE SHIP THAT DIED OF SHAME

*MIKE's flat.*

*Late at night. The TV is on.*

*PETER and MIKE are standing in the living room.*

*There is a laptop with a plastic bag of cables, sitting on the table.*

PETER: I'm sorry to come round like this.

MIKE: It's fine.

PETER: You're sure you weren't asleep?

MIKE: I was watching TV.

PETER: That's good.

MIKE: They want more people to go to the Dome.

PETER: Right. How are you?

MIKE: I'm fine. How are you?

PETER: Fine. Work's going well.

MIKE: Made a lot of money?

PETER: It's good. How are things with you?

MIKE: It's fine.

PETER: How are your options?

MIKE: They're not worth much now.

PETER: Oh. Still though.

MIKE: How's Jenny?

PETER: She's good.

MIKE: Are you guys moving in together?

PETER: Not yet. We've talked about it. How about you? Any luck on that front?

MIKE: Well, you know – It's been a bit quiet to be honest.

*Beat.*

Look, Pete, it's – (*In reference to his watch.*)

PETER: Sure. Sure. You haven't checked your email in the last couple of hours have you?

MIKE: I've been watching TV.

PETER: Of course you said. TV is good.

MIKE: You said your computer had been crashing?

PETER: Yeah. Actually, when I said that about the computer crashing –

11

MIKE: It shouldn't be crashing. That's a good machine.

PETER: You're right. It hasn't crashed.

MIKE: It's a good machine.

PETER: More of a…malfunction. It's sent out an email. To everyone in my address book. Just did it itself.

MIKE: That could be a virus. There've been some nasty worms going around –

PETER: That's not really the key point. The email had a picture attached to it. An offensive picture. I've already had a very nasty reply from a friend in New York.

MIKE: (*Perhaps the beginnings of a laugh.*) What? A female friend? You mean it sent out some porn?

PETER: Yes and no. It's worse than that. (*Beat.*) I need you to read between the lines here.

MIKE: I can't, Pete.

*Beat.*

PETER: It's pornography. But it's not…legal pornography. Even if I weren't a lawyer, I'd know it's not legal. It's not…adult. Somehow it's come down the line and it's gone out to my entire address book – a great many lawyers, a few judges, my head of chambers.

*MIKE looks at PETER*

MIKE: Where's Jenny?

PETER: She's in Newcastle. On a piece.

MIKE: Have you spoken to her?

PETER: I'm just about to. I need to ask you a big favour. If this thing's come down the line onto my computer – then, well, anything could have. Obviously I've looked but – What I'm asking is, can you really erase things? Wipe them completely?

MIKE: Sure. If you know how.

PETER: Would you do that for me? Make sure it's clean?

MIKE: Wipe the whole hard drive?

PETER: I just need the Work folder.

*Pause.*

MIKE: I'll sort it out for you.

*MIKE takes the bag with the computer in it.*

PETER: That computer must really hate me.

MIKE: It's just a machine.

*MIKE makes an affectionate gesture towards the computer – perhaps he pats it. He walks out of the room with the bag.*

*PETER takes out his mobile phone, speed dials. Gets JENNY's voicemail.*

PETER: Oh come on. Hi, it's me. Just to say: my computer's had some kind of…virus or something. Mike's sorting it out for me now, but you'll have received an email from me, I mean not from me, but from my computer. It's got some random title about good shares to buy. Just delete it. And call me. Hope you got what you wanted in the interview. Maybe you're asleep. Hope so. Bye.

*PETER ends the call.*

*MIKE comes back into the living room.*

MIKE: Did you call Dad?

PETER: I was just calling Jenny.

MIKE: He's in your address book, right? Tell him to delete it without opening it. You should do that right now.

PETER: Of course. I'm going to.

MIKE: He shouldn't see that. You should call everyone.

PETER: Of course. Is it doing it now, then?

MIKE: It's running. I was just thinking. I can't have seen you in two, three months.

PETER: It's been really hectic.

MIKE: Here you are now though. In your hour of need.

PETER: It's really good of you.

*MIKE nods.*

MIKE: Busy with work?

PETER: A big case on. I'm working with one of the QCs in my chambers.

MIKE: I guess that consumes you.

PETER: You're doing well, though? That's what I tell all my friends. You're the whiz-kid.

MIKE: It's doing my head in Pete.

*Beat.*

PETER: I'm sorry to be bothering you with all this.

MIKE: (*Suddenly.*) There aren't viruses like that.

PETER: There must be.

MIKE: I've never heard of one. Not like that. Send out a picture like that.

PETER: I'm telling you it –

MIKE: I'm not stupid.

PETER: I'm sorry if you saw that picture. It's a horrible picture.

MIKE: I'm not fucking stupid. Suddenly it's handy having a nerd for a brother.

PETER: What are you talking about? I'm proud of you.

MIKE: This has gone out to your entire address book?

*Beat.*

PETER: It's fine. You've changed your mind. I'll take the computer back and we'll forget this ever happened. It's fine.

*PETER goes over to the door of MIKE's bedroom and tries to open the door.*

The door's jammed. Have you locked my computer in your bedroom? This is ridiculous. Why do you have a lock on your bedroom door?

*PETER's mobile phone begins to ring.*

*He takes it out of his pocket, glances at the face.*

You're my brother.

MIKE: And what's that supposed to mean?

*The phone continues to ring.*

You should answer that.

*Music begins to play, possibly Rufus Wainwright, 'Cigarettes and Chocolate Milk'.*

*After a moment, PETER begins to undress.*

*After a moment, MIKE turns away.*

*PETER takes off his normal clothes and gets into loose tracksuit bottoms, trainers and a white T-shirt. His possessions are taken away, including his watch, and he is given new clothes to wear. Those doing the taking away and the giving should be brutal: this is PETER's entry into the world of prison. There is a moment when he stands before us in his underwear, exposed.*

*Music runs under this and whatever set change is necessary.*

*Into:*

## WINKING

*In PETER's cell.*

*HARRY comes in with his guitar.*

*PETER is lying on his bed, reading a book.*

*HARRY pauses at the door.*

HARRY: You're quiet aren't you? (*Looking around the tiny cell.*) On your own again?

*Beat.*

15

Fair enough, fair enough. I was quiet at first. Quiet as the bloody grave. It's a shock isn't it? Hits you like a car crash. I was quiet the first time. Didn't know where I was. Didn't know what I was. Course we're not the victims. I know that. It's not about us. Yeah. Like I'd been hit by a car. Can't stay in here forever.

PETER: Look, Harry, I said to you – I'd rather be alone right now.

HARRY: Yeah. Whatever. As the young people say nowadays.

PETER: I was reading.

HARRY: Right. What are you reading then?

*Beat.*

PETER: Pride and Prejudice.

HARRY: Good, is it?

PETER: It's incredible.

HARRY: I missed it on the telly. Saw the first episode then they took away my privileges. I was denying my guilt.

PETER: So they denied you Jane Austen?

HARRY: I was being disruptive. Different nick. Different Harry, really. From the library, is it? I'm guessing it's got a happy ending. Or have you not got there yet?

PETER: I've read it before.

HARRY: Remind you of outside, does it? People do that in here, I've noticed. Read a book to forget where they are.

PETER: It's a different world.

HARRY: It doesn't work.

*HARRY wanders about in the narrow confines of PETER's cell, while PETER sits on his bed.*

*While HARRY talks, PETER begins to roll up the sleeve of his sweatshirt to reveal a bandage on his arm. PETER looks at the bandaged wound on his arm, perhaps pokes at it or pulls back the bandage a little to inspect it.*

You should put some pictures up. She ends up with the rude good-looking one, right?

PETER: Yes.

HARRY: You could see that coming. Marvo said it was good.

PETER: Marvo?

HARRY: Marvo the Magnificent. Real name Brian. He did children's magic shows. Told the kids he had magic powers. Misused that. We talked about it in the group. Role-played it. A guy called Lionel suggested he could play the role of the rabbit. That didn't go down very well. He liked to think he was a bit of a joker, Lionel. That was his way of resisting the group. But Marvo was a good guy.

PETER: That's a relative term.

HARRY: I suppose it is. If you want to say that.

*By now, HARRY is seated on the one chair in the cell. He has his guitar on his lap.*

*HARRY begins to try to play the beginning of a song (perhaps 'Help!' by the Beatles) on his guitar. He is very bad and mumbles the words.*

PETER: Harry. I'm really not in the mood. My arm hurts.

HARRY: What's that got to do with anything?

PETER: It's burnt! It's burnt.

*Beat.*

HARRY: Of course, I'm sorry about your arm. I'd been meaning to ask you how it was.

PETER: Sore.

HARRY: Right. You know I do feel sorry about that. I do. Fat, wasn't it? You were lucky –

PETER: Lucky?

HARRY: I mean he was probably aiming for your face. I got jugged up on my chest once. Hot milk and sugar. Sticks to you, doesn't it? Like Napalm. We're talking fifteen years ago now. I lost one of my nipples actually. My own little Vietnam down there it was.

*HARRY starts to pull down his T-shirt and looks down at his chest.*

PETER: Not now Harry.

*Pause.*

It was good.

HARRY: What?

PETER: Pride and Prejudice. I saw it on TV.

HARRY: They said it was good.

PETER: It was well done.

HARRY: I'm sorry I missed it. But I can't blame anyone else for that, can I? I had distorted thinking. I can see that now.

PETER: I'm sorry about your chest, Harry.

HARRY: Men don't need nipples.

*Beat.*

You know the bastard's gone? They ghosted him. Transferred him in the middle of the night.

PETER: The PMO told me.

HARRY: It wasn't an accident that.

PETER: I didn't think chance was in the frame.

HARRY: Slip on the floor bullshit. It's non-slip flooring, isn't it?

PETER: He ran towards me screaming, 'I hope you burn in hell you fucking nonce.'

HARRY: Yeah. It'll have helped him clear his debts of course. You being a lawyer as well. And all the stuff in the papers. Some people have said you're a bit above yourself. But I've put in a good word. From an old hand. You're not as you appear.

PETER: Thanks.

HARRY: It won't count for much with those thugs out there. This place is full of nasty pieces of work. You'd be surprised.

PETER: I'm not that surprised to be honest.

HARRY: Well, you know. You need to watch out. Yeah, I was in shock my first time in. You're not going to believe this, but the first time I was up for it, the magistrate winked at me. Swear to God. I mean it was a small offence, but... Everybody had distorted thinking then, didn't they? Nineteen seventy-one. A year of distorted thinking.

PETER: That was the year I was born Harry.

HARRY: Really? Bloody hell.

*Beat.*

PETER: When I came back from the doctor, with my arm bandaged up – what did you think then? What did you feel then?

HARRY: Empathy. I felt sorry about it. Because you're a decent guy. I can tell that. Beneath the hard surface.

PETER: Really? I had a funny moment while they were bandaging it up. I felt like I was looking at myself in this ridiculous situation and it felt like it was real. For the first time, it felt like it was real. Sitting there with the nurse. I actually said under my breath: Well this is it now. It's begun.

*Into:*

## JOINERY

*ELLEN's office within the prison.*

ELLEN: How's your arm?

PETER: Healed. Thank you.

*ELLEN makes a note. Beat.*

ELLEN: I was sorry to hear about your father.

PETER: We aren't very close.

*ELLEN makes a note.*

ELLEN: How is he?

PETER: If I tell you will you note it down?

ELLEN: Of course.

PETER: He's lost a lot of his right side. But he can still speak.

ELLEN: I'm sorry. Is he in hospital?

PETER: His girlfriend's looking after him at home. And my brother helps out. He's doing well, apparently.

ELLEN: He brought you up on his own, didn't he? After your mother died.

PETER: Yes. A long time ago.

ELLEN: I could see if we could get you a compassionate licence, for a visit.

PETER: No thanks.

ELLEN: Does he not want to see you?

PETER: I don't think I've conformed to his notion of military discipline.

*Beat.*

ELLEN: Officer Ryland tells me that you've expressed reservations about participating in the treatment programme. There'll be a place available in June, here. You wouldn't have to transfer.

PETER: I'm one of the lucky ones.

ELLEN: Yes, you are. A lot of people never get a place. We're keen to have you in the group. Your psychometric scores were high.

PETER: Are you flattering me?

ELLEN: I'm not telling you anything you don't already know.

PETER: Look. I've behaved well here. I've kept out of trouble. I've never denied my crimes. I pleaded guilty. I did that already.

ELLEN: You had little choice.

PETER: But I can't sit round in a circle and…talk about all this. Go back. My head – it's a private place.

ELLEN: Is it? You can't do this on your own. The group will hold you to account. You have to listen to others and learn from what they say. You have to judge and be judged.

PETER: Or you could just put me in the stocks with a big sign.

ELLEN: We're phasing that out.

*Beat.*

Your girlfriend has asked to visit you.

PETER: Ex-girlfriend.

ELLEN: You've denied her request.

PETER: I haven't seen her since I was arrested. She was angry.

ELLEN: Do you not want visitors?

PETER: Does it look like I do?

ELLEN: Would you say you had a problem with aggression? You don't have to fight me all the way. Fight for a while, if you like. But at some point, you can stop.

PETER: I'm not fighting. I'm thinking.

ELLEN: You should watch that distinction.

*Beat.*

PETER: How have you categorised my risk level?

ELLEN: What do you think it is?

PETER: I don't know how you grade it. But I'd say low.

ELLEN: With your combination of offences, I'd say you were medium risk. Medium to high.

PETER: Medium to high?

ELLEN: It depends on how you behave over the course of your sentence. And if you do the treatment programme.

PETER: What happened with Dawn was…a one-off. I don't know where it came from.

ELLEN: It was a moment of madness?

PETER: If you like. Do people not have those any more?

ELLEN: You think you wouldn't have done it again – if fate hadn't intervened?

PETER: Well, yes.

*Beat.*

What are the statistics on all this? For re-offending.

ELLEN: You're not a statistic. What are you going to tell yourself: well, there's only a forty per cent chance that I'll start looking for pornography? Or forty-five? Or fifty? Will that help you?

*Pause.*

PETER: I was a good barrister. It may seem hard to believe in our current situation, but – I was good. Judges were beginning to notice me. Comment on what I was doing. I was rigorous.

ELLEN: I can believe that.

*Beat.*

You know the implications if you don't volunteer for the programme?

PETER: The parole implications?

ELLEN: Yes.

PETER: My PO made them pretty clear to me.

*Beat.*

Harry can't stop singing your praises. It's like it's all in the past for him.

ELLEN: Peter, I have a number of reports to write. Is there anything else you wanted to ask me?

PETER: There's so many things I don't understand about this. I mean – empathy exercises?

ELLEN: It's a muscle. If you don't use it, it wastes away.

*Beat.*

All this talk about privacy is a red herring. That's not your real concern here.

PETER: Isn't it? Then what is?

ELLEN: Why don't you work that out?

*Into:*

## JENNY VISITING

*Visiting room at the prison.*

*Though this may not be represented, the room would be quite busy and noisy with other visits. Prison Officers patrol up and down to prevent the passing of contraband. JENNY and PETER's privacy is limited – we may imagine that they will quite often look about them, to check whether they are being listened to.*

*PETER is already waiting at a table. He is seated. He may be wearing a brightly coloured sash or vest in order to identify him as a prisoner and not a visitor.*

*Enter JENNY. She is dressed more soberly than before, perhaps in a suit. She looks older.*

*Beat.*

*JENNY approaches the table.*

*PETER stands up as if to offer her a seat.*

*JENNY does not move.*

PETER: Please, sit down.

*JENNY does not move.*

JENNY: Well here we are.

PETER: Yes.

JENNY: You sit down.

*PETER sits down again.*

*JENNY remains standing.*

I meant everything I said. In my letter.

PETER: I know.

JENNY: I meant every word. Excuse me.

*Beat.*

I don't have to be here.

PETER: I know.

JENNY: Nobody wanted me to come to see you. My mum thinks I'm mad. All my friends, especially the ones who got the email – Actually I – I think I may have to leave.

PETER: Please. It's good to see you. Wait a moment. I'm sorry I took so long to reply to your letter. I needed time to think. I couldn't bear to see you.

JENNY: There's part of me that's amazed I can bear to see you.

*Beat.*

*JENNY sits down on her chair.*

PETER: So how are you?

JENNY: How am I? I'm fine.

PETER: How's work?

JENNY: Fine.

PETER: Been busy?

*Beat.*

JENNY: It's been quite good actually. I've written some good pieces. Strange, isn't it, the way things always seem to go well in one area of your life when another area of your life is going to shit?

PETER: I hadn't noticed any compensatory mechanism myself. I've seen a couple of your pieces. You're right. They're good.

JENNY: Really?

PETER: The one about the frozen asylum seekers.

JENNY: Right.

PETER: The one about literary Dublin. That was really interesting. Made me want to go there. What are you working on now?

JENNY: Nothing important.

*Beat.*

PETER: I do a lot of reading. The paper, books. They have some classics in the library. Austen, Dickens. Alongside all the car maintenance manuals. I never really got Dickens before.

JENNY: Don't say things like that.

PETER: Don't say what?

JENNY: Don't try – Don't try and make it sound positive.

PETER: It's not positive.

*Beat.*

How was your journey?

JENNY: The taxi driver asked me if I was visiting a prisoner and I lied, I said I was doing a piece.

PETER: I'm sure G2 would go for that.

JENNY: Don't be disgusting.

*Beat.*

I defended you. You know that? I tore Mike apart. I said you'd got lost. That was the phrase I used. And then the police call around. Interview me. Under caution. Do I know anything about Dawn Taylor? They'd found some emails. Along with all the pictures. And then the papers start calling.

PETER: I'm not sure – I'm not sure we should talk about this now. Not like this.

JENNY: Really? What else are we going to talk about?

PETER: Everything else.

25

JENNY: Here's the riddle. One day you're an ordinary guy – I mean, you're a lawyer, but you're not a monster, that was the joke we made, wasn't it? And then next day… Could you see? Could you see that she was suffering?

PETER: Please don't.

JENNY: She trusted you.

PETER: I know. I'm sorry. I shocked myself.

JENNY: You shocked everyone.

PETER: But I can't… I can't just be that. Not here, now, with you. I can't be saying sorry for every minute of every hour of the rest of my life.

JENNY: Can't you?

PETER: I have to be able to breathe. I have to be able to walk.

JENNY: I'm not sure that's right. You should be on your knees. You should be walking miles on your knees. Something like that. Are you sorry?

PETER: I am sorry. But sorry's not much of a word.

JENNY: It isn't, is it?

*Pause.*

So that's the punishment? You just sit here reading?

PETER: And you meet people.

JENNY: You mean the other segregated prisoners?

PETER: I don't get to see anyone else now.

JENNY: What is it they call it? The Vulnerable Prisoner Unit.

PETER: Yes.

JENNY: Vulnerable. That's kind of rich isn't it?

PETER: It's Newspeak. There's a whole language.

JENNY: I know. I looked it up on the web.

*Beat.*

So have you made any friends?

PETER: No one you'd want to invite over for dinner. Actually, there's this guy, Harry, he plays the guitar like he has a personal vendetta against the instrument. You wouldn't want to eat with him either, but he's friendly. And he hasn't really got anybody.

JENNY: No visitors?

PETER: That's not unusual. You'd be surprised how many people never get to sit in this beautifully decorated room.

JENNY: And what did this Harry do?

PETER: People in here don't talk about that so much.

JENNY: I'm not in here.

PETER: He's been in and out of prison all his adult life. About ten years ago he started going out with a woman with a daughter. I think it was going on for a number of years. And then the mother decided she'd had enough.

JENNY: It?

PETER: You want me to spell it out?

JENNY: Maybe I do.

PETER: If we said everything that could be said, we'd drown in it.

JENNY: Perhaps we should drown in it.

*Beat.*

I'm sorry about your dad.

PETER: I'm sorry about my dad. Mike told you?

JENNY: He sent me an email.

*Pause.*

PETER: What's it like out there?

JENNY: What do you mean?

PETER: How's London?

JENNY: Grey and wet.

PETER: Noisy?

JENNY: Yes.

PETER: Red buses?

JENNY: Still red. Is that what happens? You forget what it's like? Everything's there. Surviving. I've started running again.

PETER: That's good.

JENNY: It empties my head.

*Beat.*

I was wondering how you'd look.

PETER: And how do I look?

JENNY: The same.

*Into:*

## THE GUITAR

*PETER is in his cell. He is using a hacky-sack, trying to see how many touches he can make, keeping the ball up.*

*Enter HARRY. He stands watching PETER for a moment.*

HARRY: You're getting good at that. Clever of your friend to give you that, wasn't it? I was never much at football. Lot of the boys used to play very rough when I was a kid.

*HARRY watches.*

You have to concentrate quite hard, don't you?

PETER: (*Concentrating.*) Yes. (*The hacky-sack drops.*)

HARRY: You're pretty good. I'm surprised.

PETER: Thanks a lot. I still – I used to play on Sundays sometimes. Pub league.

HARRY: I've got two left feet.

PETER: Maybe you should try again. On the outside.

HARRY: Wasting my time. I just wasn't built for it. Good visit was it?

PETER: Fine.

HARRY: That's two visits.

PETER: I didn't think she'd come again. But she did.

HARRY: She's a good friend to you isn't she?

PETER: Yes, she is. It's strange.

HARRY: Makes a difference, that.

*Beat.*

PETER: How are you Harry?

HARRY: Well the weather's nice, isn't it? Always picks me up, even from the window. And I sent off that letter to the clinic.

PETER: Ellen signed it?

HARRY: (*Nods.*) Thanks for taking a look at it. I appreciate it. You must be busy.

PETER: Busy? When will you hear from them?

*HARRY shrugs. PETER starts kicking the hacky-sack again.*

HARRY: When the wheels turn, so to speak. Just got to wait, haven't you? Beautiful day. In the meantime. How are you sleeping?

PETER: Better than it was. All right.

*PETER carries on kicking the hacky-sack for a few moments.*

HARRY: What do you think of Tim Piers?

*PETER stops kicking the hacky-sack.*

PETER: What?

HARRY: You know. Tall guy. [*Change line as necessary.*]

PETER: I know who he is.

HARRY: Well, him.

29

PETER: You know what I think of him.

HARRY: We were just talking.

PETER: You shouldn't talk to him.

HARRY: Just talking, that's all.

PETER: I don't want you talking to him.

HARRY: I can talk to him if I want.

PETER: They're never going to lower the age of consent.

HARRY: But they already did. Just the last few years, didn't they?

PETER: Not enough for him.

HARRY: What about Holland?

PETER: Show me the tulips. Holland is Holland. And anyway, I'm sure it's not how he'd want it. Even in Holland.

HARRY: He's always refused to do the course. He said it would do something to his human rights. I said he was suffering from cognitive distortions and he just laughed at me. He said he was taking pills for his cognitive distortions and he was feeling much better.

PETER: Very amusing.

HARRY: He said it's just a bunch of middle-class people lecturing us about things they don't understand.

PETER: I'm middle class.

HARRY: Not any more. You're one of us.

*Beat.*

He's just talking.

PETER: You might get Cat C any time now. Isn't that what Morgan said? You listening to Piers would screw your parole assessment. He'd screw it right up.

HARRY: He said you were trying to control me.

PETER: He said what?

HARRY: He told me to ask you why you were being so nice to me. Why would anybody be nice to me, he said. I said we have a good natter. I said you were my friend. That's right, isn't it?

PETER: Sure. Tim Piers is...

HARRY: What is he?

PETER: He's not helping you.

*Beat.*

HARRY: He gave me some stuff.

PETER: Some of his literature?

HARRY: There are scientists, they say it's not so harmful or something. Proper scientists, not screws. Shrinks.

PETER: I don't think so.

*HARRY shrugs.*

But there are going to be searches. Because of Piers.

HARRY: I know. I know.

PETER: So have you got rid of it?

HARRY: I can't.

PETER: Flush it down the toilet for God's sake.

HARRY: It's not as simple as that.

PETER: Yes it is.

HARRY: I've got pictures too. Not bad stuff. One or two of Amanda. You know I'm not supposed to have those, but I –

PETER: You've got pictures?

HARRY: Just one or two. I mean, what if they don't search us?

PETER: Where have you been keeping this?

HARRY: In the guitar. Taped up.

PETER: But that's –

HARRY: It doesn't affect the sound at all.

31

*Beat.*

PETER: I thought you were clean. What the hell are you doing with this stuff?

HARRY: Don't be hard on me, Pete. I am, you know, fighting the good fight and all that. It's…what if I said goodbye to everything? That's difficult. You must understand that. It's just a few things. One or two catalogue pictures. One of Amanda on the beach. In a swimming costume. (*Suddenly.*) You could sort it out.

PETER: Oh no.

HARRY: I want to do it, but –

PETER: Just get rid of it.

HARRY: When I try to bring it out, I can't. It's strong. You know how strong it is.

PETER: No I don't.

HARRY: I'd feel like I was killing something.

*Beat.*

PETER: Bring me the guitar.

HARRY: Somebody said to me they can tell if you put stuff down the toilet. They can collect it or something.

PETER: If anyone asks you, say you're going to play me a song.

HARRY: Nobody'll believe that. They know how much you hate my guitar.

PETER: Tell them you're trying to change my mind.

HARRY: You know they'll take all your books and everything if you get [caught]… I'll…

*HARRY walks out of the cell.*

*PETER goes to his door, looks out, comes back in.*

*Sits back down on the bed.*

*HARRY returns with the guitar.*

*He hesitates a second before giving it to* PETER.

There you go. It's all in there.

PETER: That's good.

*HARRY stands there looking at* PETER, *waiting for* PETER *to do something.*

Leave it to me. I need to think a moment.

HARRY: Right, right.

*Beat.*

How's the programme going?

PETER: Just making our introductions. Thanks for asking.

HARRY: You'll get a lot out of it. Put your head in order.

PETER: You've done well Harry. It'll be OK.

*Beat.*

HARRY: There's er…there's actually a couple of – there's a couple of – well you'll see. I'll leave you to it.

*HARRY walks out of* PETER's *cell.*

*PETER goes up to his cell door. Pushes it to.*

*Sits back down on the bed.*

*Has the guitar laid across his lap.*

*Into:*

## CARROTS

*The canteen.*

*Noise of a kitchen, chatter, people eating.*

*TIM is sitting alone at a table, eating.*

*PETER comes up to him. He does not have a tray of food.*

PETER: I want to talk to you.

TIM: I'm eating.

PETER: I'll do most of the talking.

TIM: I suppose that's what you're used to.

*PETER looks over at the prison officers who are watching over the canteen.*

Afraid of what the screws will make of it?

PETER: They can make of it what they like.

*PETER sits.*

TIM: Would you like some carrots?

PETER: I want you to stay away from Harry.

TIM: Sausage?

PETER: I don't want you talking to him.

TIM: Mashed potato?

PETER: I'm not hungry.

TIM: Lost your appetite? Or are you too much of a gourmet?

PETER: What do you want from him? He's no use to you.

TIM: I don't want anything from him. I'm trying to set him free.

*Beat.*

PETER: This stuff you've been telling him. It's wrong.

TIM: Distorted thinking? They teaching you well are they?

PETER: I don't mean morally wrong. I mean incorrect.

TIM: You read my article?

PETER: Before I flushed it away. Yes.

TIM: Well I'm flattered that you read it.

PETER: You're obsessed with the way those three scientists were targeted and criticised.

TIM: They threatened to cut their funding.

PETER: But that's irrelevant.

TIM: They passed a motion in congress. A motion in congress! To condemn a paper in a major scientific journal. What does that look like to you?

PETER: Just because it's a witch-hunt doesn't mean the witches don't exist.

TIM: I didn't say 'witch-hunt'. That's a cliché.

PETER: The fact that an argument is unfairly treated doesn't make it a good argument. It has no bearing on the question.

TIM: That paper terrified them.

PETER: Maybe it did.

TIM: That's the great taboo isn't it? Child-adult sexual contact is always harmful. Catastrophic. Everybody has to agree with that. But when you actually look at the studies, the psychological studies, where they ask people what ill effects they've suffered, lots of them are fine. Poof! Whole thing goes up in smoke.

PETER: And so?

TIM: Children are sexual beings. Of course they are. We all know what it was like being young. Half the bloody population have sex before they're sixteen. And then you grow up and you forget it all. The age of consent isn't about protecting children. It's about denying their sexuality.

PETER: The age of consent is like the speed limit.

TIM: Exactly. It's arbitrary.

PETER: Of course to a certain extent. I read your piece. People mature at different rates. That's a banal observation.

TIM: Banal?

PETER: (*Carrying on.*) My analogy is this. We all know that people driving over seventy don't always cause crashes but we think that on balance people driving fast causes harm. So we make an arbitrary law. It doesn't matter that some academic paper argues that children sometimes have sexual encounters with

35

adults and have no particular ill effects. It's enough that such encounters are often harmful.

TIM: Don't get me wrong. I don't like child abuse. I hate cruelty to children. That's what should be illegal.

PETER: You can't give children the right of consent. Even just on pragmatic grounds. Have you ever been to a rape trial? Have you ever watched the viewpoint of an adult – an adult – being taken apart? You can't do that with a child. It's just not possible.

*Beat.*

TIM: Thank God for someone rational at last! Most of the debates I get into are nothing like this. Normally there's disgust.

PETER: You do disgust me.

TIM: Not enough though. Not in your stomach. You can still think straight. I could have been a lawyer. If the laws were different.

PETER: I don't want you to speak to Harry again. He's going to transfer to a Cat C very soon.

TIM: He's exchanging one prison for another.

PETER: He's got a chance.

TIM: If you want to call it a chance.

PETER: I want to call it a chance.

*Beat.*

TIM: They kept on giving me confinement in the last nick. Try to bring me into line. They think loneliness will keep us in order. But if you can handle the loneliness, you can do anything. Prophets have always been lonely. Look at Nietzsche.

*Beat.*

PETER: What did you do, Tim?

TIM: I don't make any secret of that.

PETER: No, I mean, what was your job, outside? You must have had one.

TIM: I was a reporter. Same as now. On a local paper. Cat in tree type rubbish. That was before I realised what my mission was.

PETER: Still. That's something else you could do.

TIM: I've always been political. When I was eighteen I ran a campaign to save a local church from being turned into flats.

PETER: You're not religious?

TIM: God no. I hate priests. But these property developers – they were total wankers. No respect for history.

PETER: Did you win?

TIM: (*Shakes his head.*) It's the establishment isn't it? Always the same. We used to go on Pride marches in the seventies. Man-boy groups. They used to respect us for our teaching. Initiating. But one sniff of power – acceptance – and they kicked us out. Sir Ian McKellen. You know you're fucked when that happens.

*Beat.*

PETER: He's not as strong as you. If he screws it up this time he'll be a pensioner by the time he gets out.

TIM: A compliment from the iceman.

PETER: You want to argue with someone, argue with me.

*Beat.*

TIM: All right.

PETER: You'll leave him alone? Let him get out of here?

TIM: Sure. He's probably too far gone by now. They've rewired his brain. Think of it as a gesture of friendship.

*PETER makes to go.*

They say people like you and me should never eat carrots in the nick. Because you can't see if they've been pissed on. But I love carrots. Always have. I'm not going to let a little piss stop me.

*Into:*

37

## ACTIVE ACCOUNTS

*A semi-circle of chairs facing the audience. There might be a block of A1 paper on an easel, with some marker pens. ELLEN and PETER are sitting in the circle. The actor who plays MIKE doubles as another offender in the treatment group, PATRICK.*

*PETER is in the hot seat.*

ELLEN: So you met her at the British Museum?

PETER: Yes.

ELLEN: Where you'd met her how many times by now?

PETER: Twice before.

ELLEN: You said in your brief account that you used to go there for lunch regularly. Why was that?

PETER: It was near my chambers. I like the atmosphere.

ELLEN: No other reason?

*PETER remains silent.*

Anyone else like to comment?

*Beat.*

PATRICK: The children, ma'am. It'd be full of schoolchildren wouldn't it?

ELLEN: Yes it would. Thank you, Patrick. That's a good comment. Would you say that was part of the attraction, Peter that you could look at the schoolchildren going round the museum?

*Beat.*

PETER: Sometimes. But I did used to look at the exhibits and… forget it.

ELLEN: Would you like to go on with your account now, adding in something about why you told Dawn to meet you at the British Museum?

*Beat.*

PETER: (*Looking down at a hand-written account he has in his lap.*)
I told Dawn to meet me at the British museum, next to a
particular mummy. I used to go there quite often for lunch
from work. Sometimes I would look at the parties of...
schoolchildren as they toured around the museum. Dawn was
about ten minutes late I think. I said I was pleased to see her
again and asked her how she was. She said she was fine. We
were both hungry. We agreed that we would have lunch at my
flat.

ELLEN: We agreed?

PETER: She said she was hungry. I suggested that we could go to
my flat.

ELLEN: She'd never been to your flat before, right?

PETER: No. We hadn't done anything.

ELLEN: Had you planned it?

PETER: I had wondered what might happen. Of course. But it
was an impulse. My work was...boring me and she was so
enthusiastic. She was pleased to see me.

PATRICK: I bet she was. What did you give her this time?

ELLEN: Patrick. Be less aggressive please.

PATRICK: Don't let him get away with it, ma'am.

ELLEN: No one is going to get away with anything. (*Beat.*) What
did you have in your fridge?

PETER: What?

ELLEN: Did you have things in your fridge? Things that she would
want to eat.

PETER: Yes.

*Beat.*

ELLEN: So you suggested to Dawn that she could have lunch. Did
she agree straightaway?

39

PETER: No. Not straightaway. She said she had to meet her mother in the afternoon. I said that we could just have a bite to eat and that I had a present for her.

ELLEN: And the present was at the flat?

PETER: Yes. I suppose I had planned it. That's what you're going to say, isn't it?

PATRICK: Too fucking right!

ELLEN: Patrick! Remember the rules of the group. So you bribed her to come back to your flat, yes?

PETER: I bribed Dawn with the promise of a present.

ELLEN: Thank you. I think that's a much more honest account.

PETER: It was… In my head, I'd prepared a speech. I had this idea as soon as we met I'd tell her I had to go away to do a case. In the Cayman Islands or something. So I wouldn't be able to see her.

ELLEN: But you never said it?

PETER: No. I met her and I opened my mouth and different words came out. I told myself it was too public to say it there. So we walked back to my flat.

ELLEN: Did you talk on the way?

PETER: I told her a joke about the British Museum. I said that it should be sponsored by Loot, and have a big banner over the entrance to the museum saying 'Loot' and so on. She didn't get it either. So then I had to explain to her how so many of the things in the museum were basically stolen during the days of Empire. She said she thought it was a stupid joke. Then we got to my flat and I put a couple of pizzas in the oven. There was some issue about how she couldn't eat a whole pizza because she'd get fat. Then she started saying, so where's my present, where's my present? She started opening all the cupboards in the kitchen. I'd got her two tops we'd seen in Covent Garden. When we went there the last time we met.

ELLEN: Was she pleased with them?

PETER: She loved them. Particularly the purple one. I said I'd like to see her dance in her new top.

ELLEN: Do you think she knew that if she didn't dance she wouldn't get any more presents?

*Beat.*

PETER: She knew.

ELLEN: And what did you do next?

PETER: I gave her the other bag, from Top Shop. It had a pair of knickers in it. They were white with a slogan on them: 'Girls 4ever'. With the figure '4'. I told her I wanted her to dance in what I'd bought her.

PATRICK: He's getting off on it ma'am.

ELLEN: Had you masturbated over this fantasy?

*Beat.*

PETER: You're good at this. Like a cross-examination.

ELLEN: This isn't a courtroom.

PETER: Still. It's impressive. You could have been a lawyer.

ELLEN: So could you.

*Beat.*

PETER: Right.

*Beat.*

What was the question again?

ELLEN: Had you masturbated over it?

PETER: Yes.

ELLEN: Often?

PETER: Several times.

ELLEN: And that had made it a more powerful fantasy for you.

PETER: Isn't that how it always works?

*Beat.*

ELLEN: How do you think Dawn felt when you gave her the knickers?

PETER: She seemed disturbed.

ELLEN: Do you think she was frightened?

PETER: I don't know. I suppose she must have been.

ELLEN: Why did you not give Dawn all the presents together?

PETER: I was afraid.

ELLEN: And what did she say to you?

PETER: She said she thought I was weird, but she still liked me. She said she had to go. I let her gather all her things up. She got to the door of the flat and she stood there for a moment. Then I offered to buy her the new coat she wanted.

ELLEN: And what did she say to that?

PETER: She said I was bound to get the wrong one so I should give her the money so I asked her how much a coat cost and she said…she said, one hundred pounds.

ELLEN: And what did you say, Peter?

*Beat.*

PETER: I said: 'Seventy-five'. And: 'I want you to dance with me.' Which she did.

*Into:*

## GOODBYE HARRY

*HARRY comes up to PETER.*

HARRY: To be honest with you mate, I'm a bit nervous. I won't know anyone.

PETER: You'll make friends soon enough. You're good at that.

HARRY: Just a question of finding the right people isn't it?

PETER: I'd wait before singing anything.

*HARRY nods.*

HARRY: Cat C. It'll be good. Almost normal.

PETER: Almost. It's good you're playing the guitar.

HARRY: It is difficult.

*Beat.*

Thanks for everything, then.

PETER: Don't say thank you to me. Be good.

HARRY: And if you can't be good, be careful. Something my gran used to say. Not appropriate now of course.

*Beat.*

You OK?

PETER: I'm just thinking.

HARRY: Oh, thinking. You'll be all right. I'll send you a postcard.

*HARRY sticks his hand out. PETER shakes it.*

I used to think lawyers were bloodsuckers. It's been an education.

*Into:*

## SCRATCHY

*PETER's cell. PETER is sitting, motionless.*

*TIM has come in.*

PETER: I don't want you in here.

TIM: It's a free country.

PETER: This is a prison.

TIM: I was being ironic. Should be a free country. England.

*TIM sits down on the bed.*

Malcolm X said it was the first time he felt really free when he went to prison. Because he could just read and think.

PETER: You're not Malcolm X.

TIM: If you say so.

*Beat.*

Besides, you owe me. He got out clean. No trouble.

PETER: Yes.

TIM: Sent him off to another prison to spread the good news. I will make you a fisher of men.

*Beat.*

It's funny isn't it, this environment. Working-class boy like me wouldn't normally meet someone like you. I was surprised. What you said about my paper.

PETER: What about it?

TIM: You agreed with me.

PETER: I didn't agree with you.

TIM: You accepted that child-adult sexual relations don't need to cause harm. Didn't you?

PETER: I said it's irrelevant. In terms of the principle, it's irrelevant.

TIM: Irrelevant? I'm guessing you didn't say that to Harry. Too dangerous for the hoi polloi to think about these things. Better to give them a simple rule.

PETER: Laws have to have a certain clarity.

TIM: But you accept the point in principle?

PETER: No, I… I don't want to have this conversation.

*Beat.*

TIM: Your girlfriend's a journalist, isn't she?

PETER: Ex-girlfriend, yes.

TIM: Always good to meet a fellow hack. I mean, we haven't met. But I see her when she visits.

PETER: That's none of your business.

TIM: She seems nice. I watch them from the end of B wing. As they walk in from the gatehouse.

PETER: I know.

TIM: She's nice looking. Petite I'd say. Typical bloody French to have a word for it. You ever think about that?

PETER: No.

TIM: What about your other girlfriends? They all been petite? Do you have a 'type'? Always the same tune playing in your head?

*Beat.*

Fifteen years ago I did a community therapy programme. Condition of release. I was more compliant then. We had to spend hours wanking over 'non-deviant' fantasies. Trying to retrain us. They used to lend us a tape recorder so we could prove we'd done it. Crazy days. Well they've given up on that now, haven't they?

PETER: That psychology is crude. It's been…discredited.

TIM: They gave up because it doesn't work. It's DNA. It's hardwired.

PETER: It's not just about sex. It's about emotions and decisions and –

TIM: You sound like one of them.

*Beat.*

You ever ask her to shave herself? Is that part of it for you? Hairlessness. I always think a boy's cock is like a little pink toy.

PETER: Get out.

TIM: Little shrimp of a thing. Is it the skin? That perfect child's skin? That's part of what I like. I'm not afraid to admit it. That and the enthusiasm. You can fall in love with that.

PETER: GET OUT NOW.

TIM: You've got a right to happiness too, you know.

PETER: No one's got a right to happiness.

*Pause.*

*TIM starts to leave.*

Wait. We did do it.

*TIM stops.*

It was my idea, but she agreed. I think she thought it would be fun.

TIM: And was it?

PETER: It was scratchy.

TIM: But it worked for you?

PETER: Yes. For both of us.

TIM: When it's right, it's right.

*Beat.*

PETER: I know that what I did caused harm.

TIM: You've been on the state-funded guilt-trip. How could you doubt it?

PETER: She was barely twelve.

TIM: They've gone through your memories and changed all the bloody words. Moments of intimacy, of truthfulness, tenderness. They've written them out of history.

PETER: I...I raped her. That's what I did.

*Beat.*

TIM: I had my first lover when I was ten. My father was a violent little shit. Alcoholic. Tried to give that up a couple of times. Hated queers. And this friend of the family, this friend showed me what love meant. He took me out of that nightmare and showed me what it meant to care for someone. To have intimacy. Of course they want to take that away from me too, don't they? Tell me I was abused. Talk to me about loss of control.

*Beat.*

He'd been through it all: vomiting over pictures of young men, electric shocks, hormone treatment. The full clockwork orange. And of course he tried. His family was there waiting for him with some nice girl and he wanted it. But one day he had to say: no, that's not what I am. This is me. This is what I like.

*TIM strokes PETER's head.*

What have they done to you?

PETER: You should go now.

TIM: I'm sorry we don't get on, you know. When you arrived, I thought to myself, well finally here's someone worth talking to. Too late now. They're going to ghost me again soon. I can smell it.

*Into:*

## TIME PASSING

*In three separate parts of the stage: the meeting room, the treatment programme room, and HARRY's cell, later, HARRY's room.*

*In the visiting room, JENNY and PETER sit opposite each other.*

*In the treatment room, ELLEN addresses the audience as if they were a group of offenders doing the treatment programme.*

*In the cell / room, HARRY sits with his guitar.*

*A pulse of music may run under this scene.*

JENNY: How are you?

PETER: Fine. How are you?

*HARRY is trying to master a difficult chord sequence. He is by now a passable player – he has mastered a number of chords. Two or three times he tries to play the sequence.*

47

ELLEN: Last week we completed the victim empathy roleplays. I'd like to thank you all for your work on what I know were difficult sessions.

HARRY: Bloody hell! (*He gives up on the chord for the moment.*)

ELLEN: We're going to begin the next stage of the programme with two sessions revising what we've learnt so far about your 'old me' and then making lists of the characteristics of your 'future me'.

PETER: I want you to do something for me. I need to sell my flat.

JENNY: Right.

PETER: Put everything into storage. Deal with the agents. You wouldn't have to go near it. I'd really appreciate it.

JENNY: Sure.

*HARRY plays the same chord sequence. Struggles through it once.*

PETER: I heard from Harry again.

JENNY: How is he?

PETER: They're talking about a release date. Some way off, but. And he says he's practising.

•

*Time passes.*

*HARRY plays the chord sequence successfully. Plays it again. He's surprised himself.*

HARRY: Bloody hell.

PETER: That's good news.

JENNY: She's in marketing or something.

PETER: I'd rather lost hope for Mike. How about you?

*Beat.*

JENNY: Actually, I have met a guy. He works for Oxfam.

PETER: Right. That's difficult to criticise. What's he like?

JENNY: He's very sweet. Very sweet.

PETER: That's great. Where did you meet?

JENNY: Lucian Freud. At Tate Britain.

PETER: That's a weird backdrop.

JENNY: So it goes.

•

*Time passes.*

PETER: How are you?

JENNY: Fine.

ELLEN: Just out of interest I wonder if any of you would be willing to put your hand up and say that when you go back to your cell you will masturbate over some of the stories you have heard today…? No one…? OK. I'll take that on trust.

PETER: How was her dress?

JENNY: She looked fantastic. Cream. Empire Line.

PETER: You mean Jane Austen?

JENNY: It was sort of Regency Christmas. All holly and candlelight. It was lovely.

PETER: Blimey. How was Mike?

JENNY: Grinning like an idiot.

PETER: He can only have known her for what – six months?

JENNY: About that. I took the piss out of him a bit. He said, when you know, you know. And I think Cathy feels a certain urgency. Being older.

PETER: Of course. How's my dad?

JENNY: Better than I expected. In the full kit.

PETER: He was walking?

JENNY: With a stick. You can tell that pisses him off.

*MIKE addresses JENNY, who turns to listen to him. MIKE is dressed for his wedding.*

MIKE: Few weeks ago, I spent an evening with him, watching old cine film of family holidays from twenty years ago. He asked me to get it all out. We watched Peter burying me in the sand and he said to me in his slurred speech what a beautiful boy Peter was. What a good boy. You don't have to keep visiting him you know.

JENNY: (*To MIKE.*) I know that.

PETER: Did my dad talk to you?

JENNY: Yes.

PETER: What about?

JENNY: Gerry Adams.

PETER: He's not still on that?

JENNY: He said he wasn't surprised they'd had to put the assembly on ice. These people killed his friends and now they're in power. We didn't talk about you.

*MIKE addresses JENNY again. It is later in the evening of his wedding, he is perhaps a little drunk. Again, JENNY turns to face him.*

MIKE: There's something I don't get. I've never got it. I mean...I only saw him every so often, but...didn't you – I mean you must have suspected something. Didn't you?

ELLEN: Today we're going to talk about relapse and how we deal with crises.

PETER: Did Mike say anything else to you?

JENNY: Not really. He was just you know, high on it all. The occasion.

•

*Time passes.*

JENNY: How are you?

PETER: Fine. How's Oxfam guy?

JENNY: He didn't make it. I mean we're not going out any more.

PETER: I'm sorry.

JENNY: We argued too much. We argued about Iraq. He said I was uncommitted.

PETER: He said what?

JENNY: He said I was a symbol of everything that was wrong with today's Guardian.

ELLEN: (*Appalled, showing some weakness.*) You can't say that Patrick. You can't say that. We went over this. You can't say that.

PETER: That is a ridiculous thing to say. It's a good paper.

•

*Time passes.*

PETER: They've given me my release plan. All the wheels are turning.

JENNY: That's good. Isn't it?

PETER: Something strange happens to time in here. 'Doing time' is right. You 'do time'. A barrow load of it.

JENNY: And what am I? Punctuation?

PETER: You're the streetlights in a long dark alleyway.

JENNY: You should have asked me for help. Earlier. You know that?

•

*Time passes.*

HARRY: Hope you like the postcard. Life's pretty good here. The attitude's not great mind you. Some of the staff could be screws, coming into your room without knocking whenever, all curfews and that. But it's a beautiful town and I'm keeping to the straight and narrow. I've got some work in a warehouse where the boss didn't seem to mind my record and no one else knows. I've played in a couple of open mic nights in pubs.

PETER: How are you?

51

JENNY: Fine. How are you?

PETER: Fine. Thanks.

*PETER gets up from the table where he has been sitting with JENNY. ELLEN gets up from the treatment programme room.*

*They meet. ELLEN hands PETER his clothes.*

I had a postcard from Harry. From the hostel in Bath. He seems to be doing really well.

ELLEN: Yes.

PETER: He's been playing open mic nights in pubs.

ELLEN: In front of an audience?

PETER: So he says. How long have I been in here?

ELLEN: Three years. Good for Harry.

PETER: Good for Harry.

ELLEN: Ready to go then? You've signed for everything?

*PETER nods.*

ELLEN: Don't come back.

PETER: Thanks.

*They shake hands.*

*PETER takes a single step forward.*

*Bright light opens up. Blinks in the light. Walks forward. Stops. It is a cold January morning.*

Christ.

*Walks back.*

Sorry, which way did you say it was to the train station?

*End of Act One.*

*There should be a substantial transformation in the look of the play between Acts One and Two, reflecting the move from the world of the prison into the outside world.*

# Act Two

## OPEN MIC

*A pub in Bath. The previous act has just finished.*

*HARRY walks up onto the stage area, stands in front of the mic.*

HARRY: Well…er. It's good to be back here at the Sailors. Erm. I'm going to start with a song that's a favourite of mine. Oh hold on.

*HARRY realises that his plectrum has fallen out from where he had it jammed under the strings on his guitar.*

Erm. This is embarrassing. (*He searches his trouser pockets, finds his spare plectrum.*) Always carry a spare.

So. I'm going to start with a favourite song. It's a song about –

*HARRY stops talking, because he sees someone in the audience advancing towards him.*

Oh. Hello. Hello, Bundle.

*Into:*

## FATHER THAMES

*JENNY and PETER are standing on the South Bank, looking out over the River Thames.*

*A warm late spring day. The river is sparkling in the sunlight.*

PETER: It's beautiful isn't it?

JENNY: Yes.

PETER: I'm sorry to have dragged you –

JENNY: It's fine. I'll have to be getting back soon.

PETER: This whole area – I've been down here a few times actually.

JENNY: Really? You never used to –

PETER: Suddenly I find I like the idea of it. The river. I guess it's the open space.

JENNY: They were talking about doing a beach, like in Paris, but the council said no.

PETER: That's a shame. I spent the whole afternoon on one of those boats when I first got out. Miserable weather as well. The crew thought I was some kind of nutter.

*Beat.*

That's another thing. People walk past. They're completely indifferent. It makes me want to shout out my name.

JENNY: Go on then.

*PETER gathers himself to shout but then stops at the last moment.*

PETER: It's not the right moment.

*Beat.*

*JENNY fishes a Waterstone's bag out of her bag.*

JENNY: I got you this.

*PETER pulls out the Cambridge Guide to Copy-Editing.*

It's the best one apparently. I asked around at work.

PETER: Thanks.

JENNY: Tells you when to use italics.

PETER: Thank you. In italics. That's really thoughtful.

*Beat.*

JENNY: Did you send the cheque to Harry?

PETER: Couple of weeks ago.

JENNY: He's not in…?

PETER: He just needed a few things from IKEA.

JENNY: It's good of you to do that.

PETER: Money's OK. Thanks to you sorting out my flat.

JENNY: Still. It's good of you.

PETER: So I keep telling myself. He's kind of impassive, isn't he, Father Thames?

JENNY: Look I should –

PETER: Wait a moment.

JENNY: I really need to –

PETER: I know. I just wanted you to see the river.

*Beat.*

How's the new boss, by the way?

JENNY: Hard-nosed and sharp-eyed.

PETER: He's an eagle?

*Beat.*

JENNY: It is lovely, the river. Sort of moving but not. I don't think I've really looked at it before. Maybe I should write about it.

*PETER reaches out and puts his hand on JENNY's upper arm.*

PETER: Thanks for coming.

*PETER lets his hand drop.*

JENNY: I should get back.

PETER: Of course.

JENNY: What are you doing later?

PETER: I was thinking of a matinee.

JENNY: It's different meeting out here, isn't it?

PETER: Yes.

JENNY: It's not how I expected.

PETER: There's no table. No crappy tea. No Kit-Kats.

JENNY: No prison officers. It's different.

*Beat.*

PETER: There was a guy inside told a story about how when he got out he used to spend hours travelling on the buses. Getting on and off at random. I thought he was making it up.

JENNY: I'm glad you're OK.

PETER: Thanks for the book.

*JENNY reaches forward and kisses PETER on the cheek. It is the first time they have kissed at all in over three years. It is a goodbye kiss, but more tender than it ought to be.*

JENNY: I'm sorry.

PETER: Don't apologise.

JENNY: Well, happy birthday.

*Into:*

## HOPE

*At the dogs in Bristol. Some background noise, commentary dimly heard over the Tannoy as a race is run.*

*HARRY and PETER come and sit down. PETER is carrying two pints. HARRY has the programmes for the evening's races.*

PETER: You sure you only want a shandy?

HARRY: Yeah. Safer, isn't it?

*For a moment they sit watching the end of a race.*

Oh bollocks.

PETER: Not yours?

HARRY: They're not running to form.

PETER: Do they normally?

HARRY: Sometimes they do. Otherwise they wouldn't print it in the bloody programme would they?

PETER: You're the expert.

HARRY: I am?

PETER: Compared to me, you're the expert.

HARRY: Nice just to see the dogs though isn't it?

PETER: They're a bit blurry, but...

*Beat.*

I thought I was going to hear you play.

HARRY: No, no. Not right now. I broke a couple of strings.

PETER: Oh right.

HARRY: I can play it now. Not like before. I'm sorry about some of those times before.

*Beat.*

*PETER looks about him.*

PETER: It's good not to be in the nick, isn't it?

HARRY: Oh yeah. Freedom.

PETER: All this space.

HARRY: Everybody's got mobile phones. That was the first thing I noticed.

*Beat.*

It's good to see you, Pete.

PETER: It's good to see you.

HARRY: You lose people in prison. People move about and leave and come back. I'm glad we've stayed in touch.

PETER: I'm glad you've got yourself a place here and...you seem to be doing well.

*Beat.*

HARRY: Actually, I wanted to talk to you about something.

*Beat.*

PETER: Spit it out.

HARRY: Well, I've met a girl.

PETER: Really? That's great. That's amazing.

HARRY: No, I mean I've met a girl.

PETER: What?

HARRY: Nothing's happened. One of the schools a lot of the kids go to this café after school and I've been sitting there sometimes, you know.

PETER: What have you done?

HARRY: I haven't done anything. I haven't really spoken to her I mean I've made the odd joke as I'm passing but nothing. The programme's still in place isn't it?

PETER: Why were you in the café?

HARRY: It's fine. It's fine. Chance really.

PETER: There's no such thing as chance.

HARRY: I'm having a bit of a crisis. But I know I'm having a crisis. So I'm better prepared.

PETER: How many times have you been to this café?

HARRY: I like the coffee. A few times. She's such a lovely girl. You must sometimes see a girl and –

PETER: Don't say that, Harry.

HARRY: You must sometimes –

PETER: Have you told them about this?

HARRY: They'd breach me.

PETER: They might not.

HARRY: You think so?

PETER: Is this why you were so keen to see me?

HARRY: Next race is coming up. Do you want to look at the –

PETER: For God's sake, shut up. I could fucking hit you. I could fucking hit you.

HARRY: Why don't you?

PETER: Why are you so...weak? What is it?

HARRY: I'm not weak, I just –

PETER: You bend in a breeze. I can't understand it. I've tried to help you and – you're like a...

HARRY: I can't go back inside. I can't stand all the locking and unlocking. If I go in again, I'll be an old man.

PETER: Then go to a different café.

HARRY: You think I can do that?

*HARRY looks at PETER. Pause.*

One time I asked Officer Ryland if he believed in people being cured and he said it's only over when you're lying on your deathbed and you know that you haven't abused again. And then he says, course in your case Harry we'd probably want to check your coffin, make sure you haven't got someone down there with you. Making a joke you know. He shouldn't've said that, should he?

PETER: It's always going to be there inside you. Thrashing away. It wants its day in the sun, same as everyone else.

HARRY: Is that what you think?

PETER: Either you go to the café or you don't. The rest is just excuses.

HARRY: I'll do it for you then. Fight the good fight.

PETER: You have to do it for yourself.

HARRY: For myself. Right, right. Of course.

*Beat.*

PETER: I had it all destroyed. Everything from my old flat. All the books. The furniture. The bed. I had it taken out of storage and then incinerated. Cost me about two hundred quid. I wanted to know it was all gone. The past is gone.

*Perhaps here an announcement over the Tannoy.*

HARRY: The race now. Let's watch the race.

*Sound of the race beginning. The dogs rush out of the traps. For a moment we are in the race with the dogs, the noise getting louder as they hurtle round the track.*

*The two men watch.*

*Into:*

## SHORT CALL

*PETER has telephoned MIKE.*

*An absurd mobile phone ring tone: The Great Escape theme perhaps. MIKE pauses before he will answer the phone, as if it frightens him.*

MIKE: Hello.

PETER: It's me.

> *Beat.*

> What did he say?

MIKE: He won't see you.

PETER: Right. You asked him?

MIKE: Yes.

PETER: Why – why won't he see me? I mean –

MIKE: Why would he want to see you?

PETER: I don't know.

> *Beat.*

> Thanks for asking him.

MIKE: He cried.

> *Beat.*

> I did the right thing.

PETER: What?

MIKE: With your computer. That was the right thing.

> *Beat.*

PETER: Bye then.

*MIKE ends the call.*

*Into:*

## HITLER

*A café in London.*

*ELLEN and PETER are both drinking coffee.*

PETER: Do they know who he is? The doctors and nurses?

ELLEN: They'd have to tell some people, for security. But not everybody.

PETER: Poor Harry. They must think he's some kind of masochist.

ELLEN: He sounded surprisingly upbeat. He likes the attention. He said he was sorry he'd let me down. Let the course down.

PETER: I should visit him.

ELLEN: I don't think that's a good idea right now. People are on edge.

PETER: You're going to take him back inside?

ELLEN: I can't discuss that with you. I wouldn't be directly involved anyway.

PETER: I think it would kill him – to go back.

ELLEN: That's not our primary concern. As you know. (*Beat.*) He's lucky he passed out before he could finish the job. He could have bled to death.

*Beat.*

How have you been?

PETER: I'm keeping away from the kitchen knives, if that's what you mean.

ELLEN: Are you working?

PETER: I've started proof-reading. And copy-editing. I did a correspondence course.

ELLEN: Do you enjoy it?

PETER: I get to correct other people's mistakes. It's very satisfying.

ELLEN: Are you meeting anyone new?

PETER: What do you think?

ELLEN: You can do it, if you want to make the effort.

PETER: And provided I tell them of course.

ELLEN: Of course. What about your ex-girlfriend, who came to visit you?

PETER: I've seen her a few times.

ELLEN: You seem to be doing well. What about your fantasies? How are they?

PETER: I don't have to talk to you about my fantasies. Not in a bloody café.

*Beat.*

I find you attractive. For the record.

ELLEN: That's not exactly what I meant. But therapeutically, it's an encouraging sign.

*Beat.*

PETER: I keep on thinking about that bloody song, from the war, about Hitler and the Albert Hall. It's terrible but I can't get it out of my head now…I didn't think he could do something like this. I'm almost impressed.

ELLEN: Harry said he saw you a couple of weeks ago.

PETER: We went to the dogs.

ELLEN: What did you talk about?

PETER: His new flat. The form.

ELLEN: Did he seem upset about anything?

PETER: What do you mean?

ELLEN: You don't think he was having any problems?

PETER: I'm sure he was having problems. He wouldn't be human if he wasn't having problems.

ELLEN: But nothing that would make him try to castrate himself?

*Beat: PETER smiles.*

Why are you smiling?

PETER: I was wondering a moment ago why you hadn't just told me over the phone. Now I get it. You wanted to look me in the eye.

ELLEN: What were you expecting? A social call?

PETER: I thought maybe you were worried how I'd take it. Or maybe you wanted the pleasure of my company.

ELLEN: I was in town for a conference.

PETER: It must have shaken you up. One of your star pupils.

ELLEN: It's certainly shaken you up, hasn't it? Anyway, Harry isn't a star pupil. He's a longshot. He's a keep-you-awake-at-night longshot.

*Pause.*

You remind me of my son. He can be pretty stubborn sometimes.

PETER: I didn't know you had a son.

ELLEN: You aren't meant to know.

PETER: How old is he?

*Beat.*

ELLEN: Fifteen.

PETER: Is he a good boy? In spite of his terrible stubbornness?

ELLEN: He's got a good heart. And actually I admire his stubbornness.

PETER: You understand where it comes from.

ELLEN: He knows what he wants.

PETER: It must be difficult for you, given what you do, watching him grow up.

ELLEN: I know how to protect him. I've taught him to be aware.

PETER: That's not what I meant. Everything you see, you hear – do you never fear that he might become one of us?

ELLEN: That's one hell of a question. He's a good boy.

PETER: But if he did, would you still love him, do you think?

ELLEN: In my experience, it can go either way.

PETER: But would you?

ELLEN: You don't get to ask me that.

PETER: I'm just wondering…what it would be like. As a parent.

ELLEN: He knows he can always talk to me. About anything. He would talk to me.

*Beat.*

How is your father?

PETER: He has good days and bad days, apparently. He's forgetting tiny bits all the time.

ELLEN: I'm sorry.

PETER: The thing is, he isn't forgetting the right bits.

ELLEN: Have you told your supervisor about this?

PETER: Of course.

*Beat.*

ELLEN: Did you think he was about to relapse?

PETER: He was clean.

ELLEN: (*Gives him her card.*) This is my office number. You call me. If you remember anything. If you need anything.

*Beat.*

I chose to do this work. I'm here because I believe in you. Because I think you can do it.

PETER: Do you?

ELLEN: I'm an optimist, Peter. That's why I do this. Because I'm an optimist.

*Into:*

## HOME OFFICE

*We are in PETER's flat.*

*It is small, bigger than his cell but something cell-like about it. It is a former council property in Essex.*

*All the furniture is new, from IKEA and the like.*

*There is a desk set up, with a lamp, a laptop and a printer.*

*There is a thick pile of A4 sheets as well – the book that PETER is editing. A dictionary lies open on the desk. The Cambridge Guide to Copy-Editing is also on the desk.*

*There is an open bottle of beer on the desk.*

*PETER is sitting at the desk, transferring his corrections from page to screen – a laborious process.*

*A Schubert string quartet is playing quietly in the background.*

*We work with him for a moment.*

*The phone rings. The phone is not on the desk. It is some distance away, on another small table. Near the table is the box that the laptop came in.*

*He answers the phone.*

PETER: Hello?… Oh hi… It's going well I think… In double square brackets… About five thousand words to go… I actually tend to send it in on disk… I'm rather primitive. I explained to Johnny… Great… No, I'm enjoying it… Bye.

*He puts the phone down and walks back to his desk.*

*He sits down, settles back to work, fiddles with something on the desk, perhaps propping up the manuscript so that it is at a better angle.*

*The phone rings again.*

*For a couple of rings he does not answer it. Then he goes back over to the phone.*

Hi... Oh right... In Italy? What's he doing in Italy?... Fair enough... Sure... Oh right... No I can do that... I can see it's tight... It's fine. I guess I should enter the twenty-first century... Sure. Sure... OK... Bye then.

*He puts the phone down.*

*Walks straight back to the table. Does not sit down. Straightens up his papers.*

*Takes a swig of beer.*

*Beat.*

*Walks over to the telephone. Opens up the box and takes out a cable for connecting the laptop to the telephone, still sealed in a plastic bag.*

*He takes the cable in its bag and returns to the desk. Sets it on the desk, almost like a mascot.*

*Sits down.*

*Looks back at his work.*

*Hunkers down over it.*

*We watch him work for a moment.*

*Into:*

## JOURNALISM

*JENNY's new flat.*

*It is late afternoon on a Saturday.*

*JENNY and PETER have been out for lunch and ended up staying in the pub, drinking.*

*They both have glasses of whisky, drink from them.*

*PETER looks about him.*

PETER: I didn't think it would work when you described it but it does.

JENNY: You didn't say that then.

PETER: I was being polite.

JENNY: Or you're being polite now.

PETER: It's a good red.

JENNY: Manhattan Sunset.

PETER: That's what they call it?

JENNY: Yup. I asked them for Dalston Sunset, but...

*Beat.*

PETER: I mean, it's not magnolia.

*Beat.*

It's good to be in a new place.

JENNY: Apart from the recent wave of drug-fuelled gangland slayings. Did you see the graffiti on the bridge down the road? 'Please drive-by safely in our village.'

PETER: Welcome to the neighbourhood.

*Beat.*

JENNY: I flunked out of that interview. The father of that soldier.

PETER: What do you mean?

JENNY: I didn't do it.

PETER: I thought you said –

JENNY: I was lying. I was preparing the questions and...I just started to imagine going into their house, him getting angry with me, why did I need to know this, la-di-da.

PETER: Can you write the piece without it?

JENNY: (*Shakes head.*) I'm supposed to file on Monday.

*JENNY and PETER look at each other on the sofa.*

PETER: You're good at it, aren't you?

JENNY: Sure.

PETER: You have to remember that.

*PETER pushes JENNY's hair away from her eyes.*

*JENNY takes his hand away from her face, holds it in her lap for a moment and then releases it.*

If I can help... I mean, I can't imagine how I could but...

*Beat.*

JENNY: I think you know it could be so good – that's the thing – but I seem to end up writing these pieces which are – I don't know – you're always compromising, and at first I liked that because I used to be really precious about writing, at uni I found it so difficult to finish an essay because it had to be just right so it was great to be forced but now... I think I'm becoming glib. I suppose like everything there's an ideal and then there's the reality.

*They are now looking at each other on the sofa.*

*JENNY reaches out to PETER's face, runs her hand over his cheek.*

*PETER kisses JENNY.*

*JENNY hesitates at first, then responds.*

*Their kissing becomes more passionate. It is fierce between them, something long suppressed, and the reawakening of an old familiarity.*

*They are touching each other and they are starting to slip towards the horizontal on the sofa. JENNY's body comes into contact with PETER's crotch.*

*They kiss for a few more moments, then JENNY extricates herself.*

Stop. Sorry. Stop.

*JENNY moves away from PETER.*

I'm sorry. This – we shouldn't be – should we?

PETER: No.

JENNY: Fuck. I can't believe it.

PETER: It's OK.

JENNY: It's not OK. Fuck.

*Pause.*

PETER: I'm sorry.

JENNY: Why are we drinking?

*JENNY pours herself some more whisky. Drinks from it.*

I hadn't expected you to be so…

PETER: So what?

JENNY: It doesn't make any sense.

PETER: Expected?

JENNY: I mean…

*Beat.*

It's like vertigo.

PETER: I still… I still want you.

JENNY: What? What?

PETER: You're beautiful.

*Beat.*

JENNY: I know where your lips have been.

*Beat.*

My editor said to me I should write a piece about it. About you. Under a pseudonym. He's challenging me. He thinks I'm losing my nerve.

*Into:*

## **AMANDA**

*HARRY's bedsit in Bath.*

*PETER is seated. He has a cup of tea.*

*HARRY is putting an extra cushion on his chair.*

HARRY: Sorry.

PETER: Are you all right with that?

HARRY: This'll do it. (*Of the cushion.*) I got one of those inflatable things, like a swimming ring. But I was rocking about on it. Made me seasick. (*Beat.*) What did you think?

PETER: Lovely.

HARRY: They'll get bigger of course.

PETER: They're puppies.

HARRY: They'll be ready to leave in three weeks.

PETER: You're definitely going to have one?

HARRY: The coppers weren't happy with it. Typical. But probation persuaded them. Give me something to do.

PETER: You'll have a beautiful dog.

HARRY: He can look after the flat. I'll teach him to do the hoovering.

　　*Beat.*

PETER: Does probation know you're seeing me today?

HARRY: Oh yes. Took quite a lot of negotiation to come and see you. They're worried about your influence. Lot of them wanted to take me back inside. Said I was too unstable. But they've got me under close monitoring instead. I've got satellites tracking me.

PETER: What?

　　*HARRY lifts his trouser leg to show he has a tracking tag attached to his ankle.*

HARRY: They're watching me from space. They call it Managing Trust. It's like trust, but it's managed.

PETER: If you have an offending thought, it blows your foot off.

HARRY: Something like that. Yeah, then, Terry, he's the one who said I should get the dog, he said I ought to see you, you know, to say goodbye.

PETER: They said you shouldn't see me again?

HARRY: No one from prison. Not from before. Not after what happened.

PETER: And you're going to go along with that?

HARRY: It's the last chance saloon, isn't it?

PETER: I suppose it is. I'll miss you.

*HARRY nods.*

*Beat.*

HARRY: What did Ellen tell you?

PETER: Just that you'd…hurt yourself. And that you were getting better.

HARRY: She didn't tell you anything else?

PETER: No. We could still keep in touch you know. The odd phone call.

HARRY: I shouldn't.

PETER: I don't think they're bugging your phone. Not even with the satellites.

HARRY: No. It's best not.

*Beat.*

PETER: Why did you do it?

HARRY: Why do you think? I thought if I could just – What you said about the girl in the café and…I went back.

PETER: Christ, Harry.

*Beat.*

HARRY: She found me, didn't she?

PETER: Who found you?

HARRY: Amanda. My Amanda. Just after Easter. I was in the
Sailors. Doing an open mic slot. I was about to start and there
she was, in the back of the pub, standing up, watching me.
Tears running down her face. She was all grown up of course.
All made up and that. But so beautiful. Still had her hair long.
She was crying. She started walking up to me. I thought she
was going to use the mic. Tell everyone what I'd done to her.
But she didn't. She ran away. Straight out the pub. But I got
a letter from her a few days later. Care of the Sailors. It was
a terrible letter. Said she hated herself, hated everything and
that was because of what I did to her. Said she'd tried to kill
herself a couple of years ago. She said that all her food tasted
bad. I did that. I should have been caring for her and I turned
her bad.

*Beat.*

PETER: So you started going to the café?

HARRY: I was spinning about. I was off my feet.

PETER: This is all her fault now? I can't believe this.

HARRY: I'm not – She stopped, just just over there, as close as
that table as close as that. Eight years since I saw her. She just
stood there, looking at me.

*Beat.*

I'm not distorted. I'm bloody not. I needed someone to talk to.

PETER: You could have talked to me.

HARRY: Talk to you? I tried that, didn't I? I thought we were
a team or something. I thought you were on my side and
suddenly you, you were coming all moral like you're Ellen or
Mother fucking Teresa but you're not.

PETER: That's not what I meant.

HARRY: We make mistakes, Peter. We're human. We do terrible things.

PETER: You have to fight it.

HARRY: How can I fight it when I'm so weak? That's what you said, isn't it? You made out I was some kind of loser.

PETER: You were going to touch that girl.

HARRY: I needed you to listen to me.

PETER: You were going to touch that child.

HARRY: You're the only one I've got.

*Beat.*

Perhaps I shouldn't have said anything but I thought since this is it. There's hope for me. I've got hope.

PETER: I'm sorry. I should go. You should get that dog. It'll be good for you to have the dog.

HARRY: You're not my father. You're no better than me.

PETER: I know that.

HARRY: Do you? Last week, when I phoned you, it took me a while to get through. I was hanging round waiting by the payphone.

PETER: I was on the phone.

HARRY: No, no. I tried your number every ten minutes. For an hour. You weren't on the phone.

*Pause.*

PETER: I wasn't looking at anything illegal. I was –

HARRY: You were at the bloody door.

PETER: I was working –

HARRY: And then you speak to me…like I'm an animal.

PETER: I'm sorry Harry.

HARRY: Don't sorry me. Not after all we've said about sorry.

PETER: I should go.

HARRY: Couldn't you see? I was asking you for help. Couldn't you see?

*Into:*

## THE BEST EVER

*A meeting room at JENNY's office.*

*JENNY is interviewing PETER.*

*A tape recorder is running.*

JENNY: Tell me about the pornography.

PETER: What about it?

JENNY: How did you get into it?

PETER: It's a good question. I wasn't interested before. I mean, before the internet, I'd seen stuff, like every guy, all fake tans and bad acting. I'm not saying I didn't use it, but…it didn't get me.

JENNY: And the internet was different?

PETER: There was so much of it. And the search engines. The way you could ask them for anything and bang, two hundred thousand pages come up.

JENNY: Google world.

PETER: Yes.

JENNY: I'm sorry.

PETER: No, you're right. Google world. And suddenly you discover there's this whole…diversity, there are other kinds of pornography, and you never knew.

JENNY: Other kinds? You mean –

PETER: No, no. Nothing illegal. Not then. I didn't set out to look at anything illegal. I was – curious. I just wanted…youth. If you've never looked –

JENNY: I've looked. Thanks to you, I've looked.

PETER: Then you'll know. There's a whole genre – college girls, girls next door, just eighteen, barely legal –

JENNY: Which is a magazine, as well, right?

PETER: Exactly. It's in the newsagent. Playing on the edge. It's the commonest thing.

It was like you'd been released in the middle of the night into this enormous, empty library and you can just run up and down the corridors, and you know that somewhere in that library, somewhere are books that offer exactly what you want. And if you carry on looking, sure enough you start to find them and then each one of them says, why don't you have a look at this as well, just click through here and there you are, isn't that exactly what you wanted, or maybe it's just a little more than you wanted, and you think well yes, that is more than I wanted but actually it's exactly what I wanted. I just didn't know I wanted it. A couple of times I saw the sun rise, and I was still there, searching.

JENNY: You were wanking over pictures.

*Beat.*

And this was all legal?

PETER: For a long time. But there was this other layer, another district of material around it. It would be half offered to you, if you were looking in a particular way. Some of it was...borderline: young-looking girls but you couldn't be sure how young, girls in school uniforms, girls you could see in a fashion shoot, maybe. And then girls in their underwear. In swimming costumes. For a while it was like that. I don't think there was ever any one moment when I crossed the line. I mean, there must have been a moment, but... There was quite a while when I simply wasn't sure or I told myself I wasn't sure and then somehow it became obvious that I'd in fact crossed the line long ago.

JENNY: You were lying to yourself.

75

PETER: Yes.

JENNY: You must have known you'd get caught.

PETER: There were times when I was terrified. But – when you got into it – late at night – it was like I was invisible. Like I was the only person in the world.

*Beat.*

You're not going to believe me, but all the time, this is the absurdity, you're swimming through these rivers of pornography, and you're looking for something that isn't pornography, which doesn't look like pornography. Some kind of warmth, something not fake. Some kind of smile.

*Beat.*

JENNY: When did this start?

*Beat.*

PETER: Nineteen-ninety…eight.

JENNY: Ninety-eight? When in ninety-eight?

PETER: Spring.

*Beat.*

I mean, not the – just sometimes, looking at –

You worked that out, didn't you?

*Beat.*

JENNY: And when we met?

PETER: I stopped then, for, I don't know – three months –

JENNY: What? In the first flush?

PETER: I mean, it was intermittent – when we met, the whole spring, I wasn't –

JENNY: Intermittent?

*Beat.*

When did you cross the line?

PETER: I don't know.

JENNY: Was it before – was it before we went to Berlin? For example.

PETER: Berlin? It was good being away. I deleted everything when we got back. Tried to.

JENNY: But had you crossed the line?

PETER: Yes.

*Beat.*

JENNY: And what about us?

PETER: I fought it. I stopped again and again.

JENNY: But you failed.

PETER: It was too easy. When I was on my own at my flat; or when you went away or you'd gone to bed –

JENNY: I'd gone to bed?

PETER: Sometimes. Maybe I'd been drinking – I'd sit down and I'd say to myself – I'll just check my emails. That was the fiction. Then it all began again.

JENNY: You loved me.

PETER: When I said that to you, that wasn't a lie.

*Pause.*

The thing was, what I felt those nights was more intense, it was the most intense thing. I've never come like that with anyone real. It was like I was free.

I did love you. I do love you. Really as well as I think I can. But alongside this other thing, it started to fade.

*JENNY presses pause on the tape recorder.*

JENNY: It's amazing that you can be so honest.

*Beat.*

You said all this in prison?

77

PETER: Not all of it. I tried not to talk about you.

JENNY: I feel ill. Silly me. Do you want another glass of water?

PETER: No. I'm fine. What I said – what I said just then, I never said that before.

JENNY: When we kissed, when we were drunk. I could feel you. You were hard.

PETER: It's not either/or. I still –

JENNY: Don't. Don't say it.

*Beat.*

Did she console you?

PETER: What?

JENNY: Dawn. Did she console you? Did you find what you were looking for?

*Beat.*

Sometimes in sex, in bed with someone, you can have remarkable coldness. Like a moment of pornography. When it's going wrong. You don't deal with it and it'll really hurt you. The tenderness has been withdrawn. You're just looking at each other. And the funny thing is that I never felt that with you. Not once. You always seemed to be right there.

I would have wiped your hard drive. I would have believed what you said. And I would have done it. And then where would we be?

*Beat.*

PETER: I don't want to carry on this.

JENNY: I don't think in fact you have a choice.

PETER: I'm not in prison any more.

JENNY: Then walk out of the door.

*Pause.*

What was it like with Dawn?

*Beat.*

Because the thing is, you said that you'd never come like that with someone real, that was your phrase. So then I was wondering whether that means that you don't think of Dawn as a real human being. Or didn't you come?

*Beat.*

PETER: When I said 'fade', that was the wrong word. I didn't mean –

JENNY: Was it good? I'm just wondering. Was it good?

PETER: I don't know.

JENNY: You don't know? You raped a girl and you can't even tell me if you enjoyed it?

PETER: It was too complicated. I was – [afraid]

JENNY: Nothing is complicated. Yes and No, Good and Evil, Love, Not Love. The world is so simple it's terrifying.

*Beat.*

PETER: I do fight it. I don't…I disconnected my phone.

JENNY: You did what? Tell me you haven't –

PETER: No. No.

JENNY: But you were tempted?

PETER: Of course I was fucking tempted. That's why I disconnected the phone.

JENNY: You want a round of applause?

PETER: I'm…better than this. That's all I'm trying to say.

JENNY: You can always get it reconnected. BT can do that for you.

PETER: I'm not just this thing.

*Pause.*

*JENNY puts the tape recorder back on.*

JENNY: So tell me. Was it good?

*Beat.*

PETER: Yes, at first… It seemed to work. She was just lying there. Looking down and seeing myself going into her. Her whole body was one smooth surface. It was so simple.

JENNY: What about her?

PETER: I… She'd become part of the room, part of the bed. I thought she was smiling. Maybe she was at first. I'm not sure I was really capable of thought, but I felt something like: This is it. This is what I meant. And then everything changed.

JENNY: When? After you'd come?

PETER: Yes. She'd rolled away from me on the bed. Almost into a ball. She was there again. She said she felt really weird. And then she was sobbing. I had this terrible sick feeling. Like I was caught in the headlights. It was very sudden.

I was staring at her back. It was shaking. She had sunburn; she must have been out in a swimming costume or something. There was this 'U' shape of bright pink on her back and it was peeling and sore. I hadn't noticed it before.

I wanted to help her, but I couldn't move. Seeing that skin… I remember thinking I should say to her, you shouldn't go out like that without putting on suncream. You're too fair. You'll burn.

*Into:*

## THE FATTED CALF

*PETER is sitting on a wall. He is outside his father's house.*

*MIKE enters. He is carrying a paper plate with some nibbles on it.*

MIKE: I thought you should have some food.

*He puts down the paper plate on the wall.*

Aunty Alice thought you were out here.

*Beat.*

I didn't know if you'd turn up.

PETER: I'm here.

MIKE: You're waiting out here then.

*Beat.*

I saw Jenny last night at the undertakers. She went to pay her respects.

PETER: That was good of her.

MIKE: She seemed fine.

*Beat.*

PETER: And how is Aunty Alice?

MIKE: Busying herself. She was upset you came to the service.

PETER: I thought I'd managed to slip in undetected.

MIKE: You know what she's like. Radar. She said she couldn't believe you came.

PETER: How could I not come?

MIKE: She blames you for the stroke. The first one. She said to me last night you as good as did it yourself.

PETER: She said that? And what's your take on that, Mikey?

MIKE: It was a stroke. Not even you could do that. The machine malfunctions. Pure chance.

PETER: That's what you think?

MIKE: Yes.

PETER: I'm not sure I believe in chance.

*Pause.*

Did he... Did he say anything about me before he died?

MIKE: He wasn't really coherent.

PETER: Don't lie to me, Mike.

MIKE: He told me I should try to look after you.

PETER: He said that?

MIKE: A few days before he died. He said that there'd always been something wrong with you.

*Beat.*

I told him I didn't think that was true. He was just trying to make sense of it.

PETER: I was a good brother to you, wasn't I? When we were kids. Looked after you. Most of the time.

MIKE: Yeah. I resented you. That's all. You were always the clever one.

*Pause.*

PETER: It was a good service. You did a good job. Apart from 'Abide With Me'. I can't stand that hymn. It's too much. I know Dad liked it though. And you spoke well. Thanks for…not saying anything.

*Beat.*

I should have gone to the undertakers. Seen his face. I know I caused him a lot of pain.

*Beat.*

Do you want to eat some of this food? I don't think I'll be able to eat all of it.

MIKE: You can leave what you don't want.

PETER: Have a fucking sausage roll. Please.

*PETER holds out the plate of food.*

*Pause.*

MIKE: Sure.

*MIKE takes something from it. Perhaps a sausage roll or a sausage.*

*PETER himself takes something from it.*

*They both eat, looking at each other.*

*Beat.*

PETER: I'm thinking of joining a book group.

MIKE: What?

PETER: Meet some new people.

MIKE: You allowed to do that?

PETER: There are rules. I mean I'll have to tell them. In certain circumstances.

*MIKE nods.*

I was thinking…one of the last times I saw dad. Five, six years ago. He sat me down and he asked me if you were gay. He was really worried about you, wasn't he?

MIKE: I was worried about myself for a while.

*Beat.*

PETER: Do you have a photo of Sally?

*Beat.*

MIKE: Not on me.

PETER: Really? The doting father? I don't believe you.

*Beat.*

It's just a photo.

*MIKE takes out his wallet, takes out a photo and hands it to PETER.*

*PETER looks at it for a while.*

She's beautiful.

MIKE: That's only two hours after she was born. Brand new. We put that up on our homepage.

PETER: She's lovely.

MIKE: This is her at the christening.

*MIKE hands PETER another photo.*

PETER: Christening? What happened to Mike the great scientist?

MIKE: Cathy wanted it.

*PETER points to the photo.*

PETER: And this is Cathy?

MIKE: Yes.

PETER: She looks nice.

MIKE: She's at home, looking after Sally.

*PETER looks at the photos for a moment.*

This is her at her first birthday party.

*MIKE hands PETER a third photo.*

PETER: It's very sweet.

*Beat.*

I mean I don't…

*Beat.*

Does she know she has an uncle?

MIKE: She's hardly talking much yet, Pete.

PETER: No, of course not.

MIKE: She's just learning about the world. Picking things up, playing, trying things out. It's like the whole world is one big lab for her. It's the most extraordinary thing I've ever seen. She says 'Bye-bye' all the time. When she leaves a room, when she puts down a toy. We were talking in the kitchen a couple of nights back and I could hear her over the intercom, lying in bed, saying 'Bye-bye' over and over again, as she was falling asleep.

*Beat.*

We'll tell her about you some day, when she's old enough.

*PETER hands back the photos.*

PETER: Thanks. She's a lovely girl.

MIKE: She's a diamond.

*Pause: they continue eating.*

Are you going to come in then?

PETER: No I –

MIKE: You can't sit out here. It's stupid.

*MIKE gets up off the wall.*

PETER: You want me to go in there?

MIKE: Don't you think you should?

PETER: What about Aunty Alice?

MIKE: She's the least of your problems. There's half his bloody regiment in there. They've got swords on.

*Beat.*

PETER: OK. I'll just –

*PETER gets up off the wall.*

*Puts down the plate of food. Picks it back up again.*

Actually, I don't think I will.

MIKE: It's up to you.

*PETER nods.*

PETER: You go in.

*They stand facing each other.*

*Into:*

## UNDERSTANDING

*In ELLEN's office.*

*JENNY and ELLEN are sitting opposite each other.*

ELLEN: This is off the record?

JENNY: You have the letter. I'm not here as a journalist. It's strange being back in this building. A different part of it.

ELLEN: It must be.

JENNY: I'm trying to think if I ever saw you but – I don't think so.

ELLEN: I don't supervise visiting.

JENNY: Of course. It's quite something isn't it? All the doors opening and closing behind you.

ELLEN: You never get used to it.

JENNY: I was going to write something about it. But I couldn't write a good first paragraph. I think writing about it, whatever I said, somehow makes it more speakable.

ELLEN: I don't know about that.

JENNY: You must take a pretty dim view of journalists.

ELLEN: Sometimes.

*Beat.*

JENNY: I don't talk to him any more. In case you're wondering. I did – for the longest time. And then I couldn't.

ELLEN: Miss Summers, you said you had something to tell me.

JENNY: Did you see the photo he emailed out? His computer emailed out.

ELLEN: No.

JENNY: The girl in it was…eight or nine, no more than that.

ELLEN: Have you been to a counsellor?

JENNY: A counsellor? (*Smiles.*) I'm training to be a counsellor. For Victim Support. Where do you put it? All the things you hear. What do you do with them?

ELLEN: It's difficult. We have counselling sessions.

JENNY: And do they help?

ELLEN: Actually, yes. And my husband is a social worker. He knows the territory. Do you have someone you can talk to?

JENNY: Kind of. Understanding's the con, isn't it? Criminals are so fascinating. Victims are so boring. You head out looking for understanding and you get lost.

ELLEN: You don't have to understand everything. You try to understand things and you'll never leave them.

JENNY: Yes.

ELLEN: Every day, the last thing I do before I leave, I go to the ladies' and I wash my hands. I spend a couple of minutes on it, and I say to myself, I am washing all this away, I am walking out of the door, and leaving it there. You should talk to someone.

*JENNY nods. Beat.*

JENNY: So this is the face they see. Do you never get angry with them? Never want to hit them?

ELLEN: You have to stay calm.

JENNY: I wonder whether you shouldn't be angry.

ELLEN: You don't think that.

JENNY: No, I do. I'd be happier if you were angry.

ELLEN: This is the criminal justice system. It's not about anger. Anger wouldn't be…sustainable.

JENNY: No. It's so tiring isn't it? I think a lot of what gets called forgiveness is just people running out of energy. That was a line from the article. Would have been.

*Beat.*

ELLEN: I did hit a prisoner once. I was just starting to do the course. Group therapy. It was a rapist. He was talking about one of his victims, an elderly woman. My mother had died quite recently. He was enjoying it. I'd been trained to deal with that but – I got up and walked over to him and hit him with the back of my hand. That shut him up.

JENNY: Did you get into trouble for that?

ELLEN: Of course. But they let me carry on after a while, because of my mother dying.

JENNY: I'm glad you did it. Listen to me! I'm not saying lock them up and throw away the key. But…that girl in the photo. What was being done to her. How could anyone say to her – this is what your suffering is worth? In months and days? What right would they have?

ELLEN: I don't have the answer to that.

JENNY: No. You don't.

*Beat.*

ELLEN: You said you had something to tell me. Do you have reason to believe that Peter is about to re-offend? Or has re-offended?

*Beat.*

JENNY: No.

ELLEN: If you know anything…?

*JENNY shakes her head.*

I thought you –

JENNY: I'm sorry. I didn't mean to mislead you.

*Pause.*

You're still in touch with him, aren't you?

ELLEN: We shouldn't discuss this.

JENNY: He still phones you? From time to time?

ELLEN: Yes.

JENNY: You're still trying to help him?

ELLEN: Yes.

JENNY: Believing in him?

ELLEN: I don't trust any of the people I work with. But in this job, you have to make assessments. And I think he's a good bet.

JENNY: A good bet?

*Beat.*

ELLEN: People do stop offending. If it was hopeless, I wouldn't be here.

JENNY: Or maybe you're just one of those people who keeps going no matter what. Maybe you're addicted to hope.

*Beat.*

ELLEN: Prisoners are released. And so we try to make them safer when they are. That's all.

JENNY: You shouldn't talk to him.

ELLEN: I'm afraid I can't agree to that.

JENNY: He shouldn't be helped.

ELLEN: It's my job.

JENNY: He served three years. Does that seem right to you?

ELLEN: I don't set the sentences.

JENNY: It's a degree.

ELLEN: He's still on licence.

JENNY: He's free.

ELLEN: He'll be on the register for the rest of his life.

JENNY: What so you can watch over him? With your tender care?

*Beat.*

ELLEN: Is that what you're going to write?

JENNY: I'm not going to write anything.

ELLEN: I've been told that before.

JENNY: I'm not going to write anything. I'm quitting my job. I'm quitting.

*Beat.*

ELLEN: I make judgements about offenders every day. Some of them will re-offend. We know that. Sometimes we get to know the victims' names. But we carry on, because it seems like a worthwhile thing to do.

*Beat.*

JENNY: I should go.

ELLEN: This is not a soft option. Nothing we do here is a soft option.

*JENNY nods.*

It was a mistake for us to have this meeting. I'm sorry.

*Beat. JENNY makes to leave.*

JENNY: Just…hear one more thing. That's what you do, isn't it? Next time you're talking to him, I want you to remember something.

It's about me. I do have someone I can talk to. I've just started going out with someone. He's a really good person. But I have these things in my head. These moments. And I can't tell him about them. I can't tell anyone. It's when we're making love. He's touching me and it's all…fine. And then I look down and somehow, in some part of my mind, I'm small. I have no breasts, no hips, no pubic hair. I'm not a woman any more, I'm a child. My boyfriend's fucking a child.

*Into:*

## THANK YOU

*HARRY stands in front of the audience, moved, nervous. There is a cake in front of him, with a single candle, extinguished.*

*He is addressing his MAPPP – Multi-Agency Public Protection Panel.*

HARRY: Well, er, thanks very much. This has been a good year for me. Much better than before and that's really because of you who've been looking after me, monitoring, managing. Managing trust and all that. Particularly you, Terry. Patch and me would both (*HARRY reaches down to pat his dog on the head.*) like to thank you for that. We've had some funny times, difficulties, but – here we are, we got through it, more or less intact. About ninety-five per cent intact. That's something that I share with Patch. There's some cake from Terry, thanks for that, but before that, it's a bit unusual, but I'd like to sing you a song. It's a favourite of mine. It's about people you care about, and what they mean to you and just about year one of the new me. So I hope you enjoy it and er...thanks.

*HARRY walks over to the side of the room and picks up his guitar.*

Right.

*He launches into a rendition of 'Wonderwall' by Oasis. It is a decent rendition – not implausibly good, but enjoyable.*

*In the first verse he falters for a moment. But he salvages it and carries on.*

*We get to the chorus, then stop.*

*Into:*

## PUBLIC MEETING

*Central London.*

*PETER is standing waiting for a bus, reading the Guardian.*

*TIM walks past.*

TIM: Peter Marsh!

*PETER turns and sees who it is.*

PETER: Tim Piers.

TIM: What a coincidence.

PETER: Indeed.

TIM: How are you?

PETER: I'm fine.

TIM: You waiting for the bus?

PETER: Yes.

TIM: Funny being outside isn't it? I'm just on my way back from a meeting. At the ICA. I'm going to be doing a talk in their Modern Taboos season. They're going to have to hire extra security. I've been beaten up in the past.

PETER: You're like a rock star, Tim.

*Pause.*

TIM: You haven't changed then?

PETER: Changed?

TIM: Made peace with yourself. Realised who you are.

PETER: I'm working on it.

TIM: You should come to my talk.

PETER: Really?

TIM: It's about this ridiculous idea of mutuality, equality in relationships. I argue for something else, a positive relationship between unequals, in which one cares for the other, teaches the other, helps the other. It's natural for the strong to care for the weak.

PETER: I take it you've written this especially for the ICA?

TIM: The kids are laughing at us. They know more about all this than we do! Just look at them. They're surfing for porn now!

PETER: Tim –

TIM: You think this'll go down well?

PETER: No. Not even at the ICA.

*Beat.*

TIM: Seen anyone from the nick then?

PETER: Not really. I've spoken to Ellen a few times.

TIM: The witch doctor.

PETER: She gives me some advice. That's all.

*Beat.*

TIM: Shame about what happened to Harry.

PETER: How did you know about that?

TIM: Don't fret. I heard it on the grapevine.

PETER: Right.

TIM: He's still practically a saint, the prick. Nearly lost it when he found the dog, but he's a model citizen again now.

PETER: The dog?

TIM: Some kids poisoned his dog.

PETER: Jesus. Poor Harry. He loved that dog.

TIM: You don't get it, do you? There's a war on here. There are people out there who want to obliterate us. They want us not to exist. They're completely irrational. We're surrounded by lunatics.

*Beat.*

You want to come for a coffee? I've got some time.

PETER: You think we should go for a coffee?

TIM: I know we got off on the wrong foot. But it doesn't have to be like that. We could have an argument. If you've got time.

PETER: I don't think so.

TIM: Or we could talk about other stuff. Architecture. Whatever you fancy. We don't have to talk about it.

PETER: Your speech is wrong, Tim. What happened to you when you were ten, that wasn't love. Not really.

TIM: I was loved.

PETER: No, you weren't. I'm really sorry.

TIM: I know what love is.

PETER: I'm sorry.

*Beat.*

You need help, Tim. But not from me. People like me make people like you.

*Beat.*

TIM: Aren't you full of shit today?

*Beat.*

93

I'll see you, then. Good luck.

*TIM puts his hand out for PETER to shake it.*

*PETER does not move to take TIM's hand.*

*TIM keeps his hand out.*

PETER: You know I can't do that.

*TIM nods.*

TIM: Fuck off then.

*Beat.*

*Exit TIM.*

*PETER is left alone on the stage.*

*Beat.*

PETER: (*Out.*) Sometimes I can sit quite outside myself. I see myself sitting on the train, reading the paper, heading back to my flat. Fighting the good fight. It's as if it hasn't been real up until now. And then I say to myself: Well this is it. It's begun.

*The noise of a London street.*

*The End*

# Timeline

These dates are for information only. They should not be included in any programme or shown on stage.

| | | |
|---|---|---|
| 2000 | August | THE SWIMMING POOL STORY |
| | August | THE SHIP THAT DIED OF SHAME |
| 2001 | March | WINKING |
| | March | JOINERY |
| | April | JENNY VISITING |
| | June | THE GUITAR |
| | June | CARROTS |
| | July | ACTIVE ACCOUNTS |
| | July | GOODBYE HARRY |
| | July | SCRATCHY |
| | October | TIME PASSING: Section 1 |
| 2002 | June | TIME PASSING: Section 2 |
| | December | TIME PASSING: Section 3 |
| 2003 | April | TIME PASSING: Section 4 |
| | October | TIME PASSING: Section 5 |
| 2004 | January | TIME PASSING: Section 6 |
| | April | OPEN MIC |
| | April | FATHER THAMES |
| | May | HOPE |
| | May | SHORT CALL |
| | June | HITLER |
| | June | HOME OFFICE |
| | July | JOURNALISM |
| | July | AMANDA |
| | August | THE BEST EVER |
| | September | THE FATTED CALF |
| | November | UNDERSTANDING |
| 2005 | June | THANK YOU |
| | August | PUBLIC MEETING |

Peter is tried and sentenced to four and a half years in January 2001. He is on bail between arrest and trial.

Sally is born in July 2003.

# Acknowledgements

Many people generously helped with my research for *Future Me*. Thank you to John Adams (Langley House Trust), Julia Alfano, Kester Armstrong, Doortje Braeken (IPPF), Jenny Carter-Manning, Paul Clark (NSPCC), Bobby Cummines (UNLOCK), Helen Drewery (The Society of Friends), Roger Howells, Barley Birney, Matt, Sophie Page, Robert Palmer, Matthew Parker, Prof David Wilson (University of Central England), Ray Wyre (Ray Wyre Associates) and to everyone I met at HMP Grendon, particularly Dr Peter Bennett and Gina Pearse, and at HMP Whatton, particularly Grant Anderson, Phil Aspinall, Mick Caddy, Heather Clarke, Ian Lane, David Moss, Natalie Peet, Tony Powell, Mick Pykett and Anne Spencer.

The particular vision presented in *Future Me* is of course personal and my responsibility alone. I have taken some liberties with the realities of prison life and the criminal justice system for dramatic purposes. And there isn't a dog-racing track in Bristol.

Thank you to Laura Barber, Merlinda Dalipi, Samantha Ellis, Anna Richards, Jon Sen, Ben Stoll and Tom Yarwood, who commented on the play at various stages. Special thanks to Paul King, who got me started; to Robbie Hudson, who read many drafts; to Tom Morris and Nina Steiger, who made crucial suggestions; to Kate McGrath, who acted as first reader, sounding board and disciplinarian; and to Guy Retallack, who has shepherded the script to the stage.

*Future Me* started life as part of a Scratch Night at BAC, directed by Paul King and acted by Gus Brown, Morag Cross and Robbie Hudson. It was workshopped at Soho Theatre in 2005. Abigail Morris directed the workshop, with Nina Steiger as dramaturge. The cast were Paul Chequer, Georgia MacKenzie, Julian Kerridge, Philip Fox, Gina McKee and Peter Sullivan. Afterwards, I rewrote the script with the support of a seed commission from Soho Theatre. Thanks to all of them and to everyone involved in the Theatre503 production of *Future Me*. Thanks also to Will Hammond and everyone at Oberon Books.

The premiere of *Future Me* has been made possible by the generosity of Sigrid Rausing and Eric Abraham, Barbara Schwepcke, the Brown family, Anthony Arlidge, an anonymous donor and many other friends.

This script went to press before the end of rehearsals, so may differ slightly from what is performed.